Mary Jo Leddy, N.D.S.
and Mary Ann Hinsdale, I.H.M.,
editors

Faith That Transforms

Essays in Honor of Gregory Baum

WITH AN AFTERWORD BY GREGORY BAUM

Paulist Press *New York/Mahwah*

Cover photograph: Robert Lansdale, photographer for *The Graduate:* The University of Toronto Alumni Magazine.

Library of Congress Cataloging-in-Publication Data

Faith that transforms.

    Bibliography: p.
    1. Theology. 2. Baum, Gregory, 1923–   . I. Leddy,
Mary Jo. II. Hinsdale, Mary Ann. III. Baum, Gregory,
1923–   .
BR50.F364   1987   230   87-13412
ISBN 0-8091-2915-9 (pbk.)

Published by Paulist Press
997 Macarthur Boulevard
Mahwah, New Jersey 07430

Printed and bound in the
United States of America

Contents

Acknowledgements

We are grateful to Kevin Lynch, C.S.P., who welcomed this project so readily. In particular we want to thank Georgia Mandakas, of Paulist Press, who carefully saw this book through its final stages. Without her help this book would not have been brought to completion. Our thanks also to our many friends in the community of learning in Toronto who have shared in our sense of celebrating the life and work of Gregory Baum.

Introduction

There is a tradition in academia that the students and colleagues of a professor mark a special anniversary, in his or her life, with a collection of essays. *Faith That Transforms* is such a collection—written in honor of Gregory Baum's sixtieth birthday.

However, because the academic world is only one of the many worlds in which Gregory Baum lives, these essays move through (and even beyond) the strictures of academic protocol.

The essays in this collection are, in themselves, indicative of the range of interests and the diverse levels of reflection present in the writings of Gregory Baum himself. To read through these essays sequentially is to retrace the shifts in the life and work of Gregory Baum: his involvement in shaping the Church of Vatican II; his opening to his Jewish past and the world of the twentieth century; his exploration of the depths of the inner world; his expanding sense of sin and grace in society; his various insights as he viewed the world and the Church from the perspective of different people and places.

The bibliography, compiled by Stephen Schäfer, details the development of Gregory Baum's interests and commitments. The list of publications is indicative of a person who is as at ease in scholarly periodicals as he is in popular publications, who is as globally concerned as he is locally involved, who is catholic in the broadest and most committed sense.

Within himself and within his writings, Gregory Baum has brought the concerns and perspectives of many worlds to bear on one another. His resulting efforts have been creative, freshly critical and constructive.

Gregory Baum is not without his critics. There are Church people who question his orthodoxy, academic theologians who

1

doubt his scholarly precision, humanists who are puzzled by the persistence of his religious commitment. These critics are accorded a measure of credibility by those who, like themselves, chose to remain within the securities of their limited world of meaning. The contributors to this volume are neither the critics nor the devotees of Gregory Baum. The writers of these essays are representative of many whose life and thought and commitment have been enriched and challenged by this remarkable man.

Each one of these authors has learned something from Gregory Baum and each one of them has taught him something. One of Gregory Baum's greatest gifts has been his self-transcending freedom to appreciate the contribution (of thought or action or belief) of a wide variety of persons. His confident exploration of new worlds and his consistent fidelity to all that is best in the history of the past has fostered, in the contributors to this volume, a desire and an ability to respond thoughtfully and passionately at the edges of the questions of their lives and our times.

The two of us who edited this collection of essays were doctoral students of Gregory Baum in Toronto. We, and a whole generation of graduate students at the University of St. Michael's College, were inspired by his teaching and encouraged by his example. In his classroom or in his office, we learned that the struggle to understand and to communicate was worthwhile and even enjoyable. We noted the ease with which he also brought his reflective gifts to labor halls, to gatherings of every size and sort, to small groups struggling for faith and justice. He was as generous as he was disciplined with his time. He had lots to spare for those who, like us, needed only some small encouragement to make our contribution to life.

The last word in this book belongs to Gregory Baum himself. His reflections, stimulated by these collected essays, provide us with a glimpse of the unifying thread that draws together the strands of his own life and thought—the thread of grace.

This book is a work of gratitude—in honor of this gracious man.

> Mary Jo Leddy, N.D.S.
> Mary Ann Hinsdale, I.H.M.

Robert McAfee Brown

Gregory Baum: Personal Encounters

Just to show how ecumenically the encounters began, it was a Jew (Will Herberg) who suggested that Fr. Gustave Weigel, S.J. (a Catholic) and I (a Protestant) collaborate on a book about Catholic-Protestant relations, in anticipation of (and possibly as enabler for) an ecumenical thaw on the United States scene. The book was entitled *An American Dialogue,* and, thanks to the grace of God rather than political prescience on the part of its collaborators, it appeared shortly before the 1960 presidential campaign, when the nomination of John F. Kennedy made "Catholic-Protestant relations" a hot agenda item politically as well as theologically.

Gregory read the book and, on a trip to New York, took the initiative to seek me out and widen the scope of face-to-face ecumenical dialogue. (The fact that I had quoted him favorably a number of times may have greased the skids for this initial encounter, but I attribute it much more to Gregory's ecumenical zeal and the indefatigable energy with which he pursued whatever leads came his way.)

The occasion itself, rather than anything that transpired on the occasion, is what remains important for me, for in those days—the Pleistocene era of ecumenical engagement—the seeking out of a Protestant theologian by a Catholic theologian was unusual in the extreme; why after all, should those in possession of the truth spend time in the company of those committed to error? Score one for Gregory Baum as a shatterer of stereotypes.

But I do remember from the occasion one comment of Gregory's which, had it been on the lips of a Protestant, would have sounded like an accusation. On his lips it exemplified what I came to value as the directness and surprisingness of Gregory's

3

conversation. "I thought your portion of the book," he remarked, "was much more catholic than Fr. Weigel's." Whether he inflected "catholic" in such a way as to give it a small "c" or not, I can't be sure, but with whatever inflection it was for me a supportive interpretation of what I was about. (Lest the comment seem disrespectful to Fr. Weigel, any reader who recalls that happily dated book will remember that his portion took a much harder line than he was espousing within even a couple of years, as the leaven of Vatican II began to make its way into his capacious mind and heart.)

Vatican II, in fact, provided a much more extended time and place to establish an ongoing relationship with "Father Baum," as, of course, all of us who were Protestant observers at the council called him in the public and formal atmosphere of conciliar Rome in the early 1960's. Having come into Catholicism out of secular Judaism, Gregory (to return to the more relaxed mode of address that soon became ecumenically okay on all but the most formal occasions) had a special feel for those who were still officially outsiders at the council, and probably no one in the entire Secretariat for Christian Unity did more for the observers than he—which is high praise, considering that those involved in hosting the observers included men of the theological stature of Jan Willebrands, Yves Congar, Augustin Bea, Thomas Stransky and others.

Those observers who, like myself, were linguistically inept got special help from Gregory, who could move with enviable ease, and in the time it took to bat an eyelash, from English to German to French to Latin and back again, with Italian thrown in for good measure. He often translated our interventions at the weekly meeting of the observers and the *periti*—Roman Catholic theological experts who counseled the bishops on many things, including the current pulse rate of the observers.

Gregory was particularly helpful in interpreting the council's crises to those of us on the outside, who, not knowing the ways of Rome, assumed that when an impasse had been reached, disaster loomed. That may have been a Protestant way of reading the signs of the times, but within Gregory's serene view of conciliar proceedings, an impasse merely signaled the threshold of a breakthrough, and by the time we Protestants had all decided that the council was falling apart at the seams, Gregory was able to argue, almost always persuasively, (a) that whatever had happened was really for the best, (b) that out of the apparent disaster new wisdom would come to the council fathers, and (c) that the Holy Spirit would use the crisis as a means of moving the Church in more creative directions than would have been possible otherwise. While I doubt if he would be as sanguine today about creative possibilities emerging from ecclesiastical hassles within the present hierarchy, the funny thing is that, back then, he was usually right. The subsequent impact of the council as a catalyst for change is surely all the vindication his optimism needs.

Later on, teaching at Toronto, Gregory continued the sharing of his critical acumen with the rest of us, by editing and writing for *The Ecumenist,* a journal whose significance has been all out of proportion to its modest size and format.

After the council, my most important contacts with Gregory for a number of years were through his writings, and since they were copious, I continued to be informed and attracted, and felt in reasonably close touch. But I missed something. Maybe it was only between the lines, or was clearly stated in some article I missed, but at all events, when I next saw him in Toronto (where he was teaching and I was visiting briefly to preach at a Protestant church) I was totally unprepared for the theological and autobiographical bombshell he dropped in my lap: he was going to take a two year leave of absence to go to New York City to study . . . sociology.

Now if he had said he was going to Innsbruck to study with Karl Rahner, or to Jerusalem to work on Christian-Jewish relations at the ecumenical institute at Tantur, or to Rome to bone up on patrology, I would have understood that he wanted to nail down certain bits of theological furniture more securely in the living room of his mind and soul. But sociology? It was as though I had announced that I had passed up a chance to work at Tübingen or Geneva in order to study epistemology with A. J. Ayer.

In response to my queries about this unexpected move, Gregory stated concisely that the theology of the future was going to have to take the social sciences very seriously, draw on them for its analysis of what was going on in the world, and employ their categories in its own discourse, if it expected to communicate with the increasingly "secular," or at least non-theological, culture.

We left it at that. The idea was too new for me to do much more than register it as something with which to wrestle. (I could also see the whole theme of my Sunday sermon going down the drain, if he were right.) But in retrospect, of course, I am dazzled by the prescience with which Gregory had seen exactly which way the theological ball was beginning to bounce, and was positioning himself to be able to play the game when some new ground rules were introduced.

Nothing could better have prepared Gregory to interpret the subsequently emerging currents of third world theology than the fruits of his decision to become skilled in the social sciences, for this was the same path that was being trod, quite independently, by Latin American theologians, and, in different ways, by their counterparts in Asia and Africa. Gregory's skill at interpreting them, and using those newly-acquired skills in his own work, have made him one of the key bridge figures between first and third world thought.

My other times of more extended personal contact with Gregory have been of a different sort, and occurred when he (now laicized and happily married) and my wife and I taught in theological institutes in successive summers at Boston College and the Vancouver School of Theology. In both places there was displayed another side of this multi-faceted human being—an adeptness for culinary skills. This was exhibited in his ability to invite my wife and me for dinner and prepare the meal with a flare that elicited both my admiration and my exasperation—admiration that a man whose human training was in a male religious order could have so skillfully adapted to the worldly and admirable pursuit of *haute cuisine,* and exasperation that I, who should theoretically always have had at least one foot in the kitchen, remain so clumsy when it comes to boiling eggs or making coffee. So, in yet another area, Gregory becomes a role model, though in this latter department I am likely to follow reluctantly, kicking and screaming throughout.

Summing up these encounters and others, along with reading a lot of Gregory's books, I ask myself: What do I so admire about this man? And I come to the conclusion that it is his remarkable ability to be *simultaneously affable in personal relations and unyielding in personal convictions.* The term "cherubic" has sometimes been used to describe his human demeanor in dealing with people—interested, caring, solicitous, willing to help. But this particular cherub also has a backbone of steel, along with a mind of similar consistency, and when matters of import are at stake, the solicitude is for the truth, however plainspoken the words must be to make the point. Gregory can offer a devastating exposé of, say, the inadequacy of Michael Novak's interpretation of socialist theory, and yet do so, as far as I can detect, absolutely without malice. He has no need—and no apparent inclination—to indulge in cheap shots or ad hominem arguments. He is a man who is sure of his footing, and who takes people seriously, whatever he may think of their ideas.

This trait was exhibited at a recent symposium at the University of Santa Clara on the bishops' letter on the economy. An earlier speaker on the panel had made laudatory reference to a certain book on currents in modern theology. When Gregory's turn came, he said, gently and firmly, something like, "I disagree with what has been said about this book, and I cannot recommend it as the previous speaker has done. I think it is a very dangerous book because it seems to speak with authority; but its facts are either wrong, or wrongly interpreted."

From all of which I draw three conclusions: Here is a good man; he is also a good man to have on your side; and if you are not on his side, you'd probably better rethink your position, for the chances are your facts are either wrong, or wrongly interpreted.

Rabbi Dow Marmur

Holocaust as Progress: Reflections on the Thought of Ignaz Maybaum

I

A Hasidic story tells of a king who owned a precious diamond which sustained a scratch. No diamond cutter, however gifted, seemed to be able to repair the damage. But one day a jeweller came who not only restored the stone but even enhanced its value: he engraved a rosebud around the imperfection and used the scratch to make the stem.

Will God ever find a craftsman who could turn the deep scratch we call the holocaust into a rosebud and transform the seemingly irreparable damage to the Jewish people into a work of art? Is it ever possible to look at the holocaust as a prelude to progress?

Past calamities in Jewish history have been viewed in this way. The biblical prophets saw the mighty nations that afflicted Israel as God's tools in the ultimate interest of Israel. Later on, even the worst tragedies were regarded as intimations of impending messianic times. Can the same ever be said about the destruction of six million Jews and countless millions of others between 1933 and 1945?

Contemporary Jewish thinkers have largely recoiled from a theology that sees the holocaust as a positive force. They have at best pointed to some possible consolation for the tragedy, and often identified the creation of the state of Israel as a source of comfort to the bereaved Jewish people. But they have not said more than that, except for one holocaust theologian: Ignaz Maybaum. The reflections that follow, based on his writings, are cautious and tentative, but brought here in the conviction that Maybaum's contribution to modern Jewish theology should not be ignored, if for no other reason than that it is so traditional and so revolutionary at the same time.

II

Despite his ten books in English, several pamphlets, numerous articles and essays, Ignaz Maybaum is virtually unknown, even in the country where he lived during the second half of his life, England. The only scholar to pay serious attention to him is Steven T. Katz in his *Post-Holocaust Dialogues* (New York University Press, 1983), and he is less than complimentary. It is not difficult to understand the reason: Maybaum put forward a theory which, on the face of it, is open to being misunderstood as offensive to the martyrs of the holocaust and pejorative to East European Jewry which paid the heaviest price in the tragedy. Who was this man?

Ignaz Maybaum, born in 1897 in Vienna, was ordained by the *Hochschule fuer die Wissenschaft des Judentums,* the Liberal Rabbinic Seminary in Berlin, where his uncle Sigmund Maybaum was a celebrated preacher. After serving small congregations in provincial German towns, he returned to the capital and stayed there until 1939. During his six years under the Nazis, which included a spell in a concentration camp, he worked tirelessly for the welfare of the congregants he served.

He continued his pastoral activities and his writing after arriving in England shortly before the outbreak of World War II. First he gave guidance and comfort to the Jewish refugees from Germany to which his first book in English, *Man and Catastrophe* (London, 1941), is a moving testimony. Later he addressed himself to a larger British public, both Jewish and Christian.

These later works reflect something of a shift in Maybaum's religious orientation. Reared in the more traditional milieu of German-Jewish liberalism, he found its English counterpart even more difficult to take than Orthodoxy. To start with—e.g., in his *The Jewish Home* (London 1945)—he was critical of British Reform but subsequently, when he was called to serve one of its congregations, which he built up to become one of the largest in the country, he not only appreciated what Reform stood for but emerged as one of its most ardent exponents. He was among the founders of the Leo Baeck College in London, which in many ways saw itself as the heir of the Berlin *Hochschule,* and taught at that rabbinic school until his death in 1976.

Here is not the place to offer a comprehensive survey of Maybaum's writings. The biographic thumbnail sketch is only intended as background to his startling assertion that the holocaust is a gateway to progress.

For Maybaum, the liberal rabbi, Judaism was primarily faith in God, not an affirmation of Jewish identity. Steeped in the teachings of the Bible, he refused to consider the possibility that Jewish history was devoid of meaning. His starting point, therefore, was the conviction that even the tragedy he witnessed *must* lead to some higher purpose.

In an interview he gave on the occasion of his seventieth birthday, he said: "Auschwitz is the great trial. The Jew is tried, tested, like Abraham at Moriah. Those after Auschwitz who still believe in God, his justice and his mercy, are the right Jews, the remnant. Those who break down shall not belong to the remnant. The remnant is that part of the Jewish people which, like Job, remains faithful to God though he slay them." This is a succinct summary of much that is contained in Maybaum's *The Face of God After Auschwitz* (Amsterdam, 1965) and strewn across many other books: an affirmation of faith in God as the greatest challenge for the contemporary Jew; Jewish "ethnic" survival will take care of itself, for God's assurance of a saving remnant cannot be in doubt. Even the horrible experience of the holocaust does not change things but brings each of us survivors nearer to a decision whether we are willing to remain Jews or not.

Once Maybaum was ready to affirm Reform Judaism in practice, he was also prepared to take the theological consequences of his stance and openly attack Orthodoxy. His later writings contain passionate outbursts against modern manifestations of East European religiosity, be it in its Hasidic or in its legalistic forms. He did not bewail the decline of Jewish Orthodoxy, which he associated with the holocaust. Perhaps its decline would be the beginning of a renewed Judaism, the faith of the remnant.

He refused to speak of the holocaust as *sho'a,* the current Hebrew term meaning "destruction," and instead used the equivalent *churban,* because Jewish tradition has used the latter word to describe the destruction of both temples in Jerusalem, events that epitomized cataclysmic national calamities which nevertheless resulted in progress. The Hitler epoch constitutes the third *churban* and thus contains the same potential for growth, even though we are not yet able to discern it.

In the same interview Maybaum said: "The first *churban,* with which we associate the Babylonian exile, made us into a people without a state but with a mission. The second *churban,* after the destruction of the Maccabean Commonwealth, established the synagogue. For the first time mankind saw worship without animal sacrifice based entirely on the spoken word. The holocaust is the third *churban* and it, too, will lead to progress."

When pressed to be more specific, Maybaum grew somewhat impatient with the interviewer, the author of this essay: "Don't tempt me. Don't force me to give you a philosophy of history. Hope is not calculation. You must never force me to specify my hopes." But he relented and added: "Were I to succumb to the temptation, I could point to the fact that after a thousand years of German oppression, the Slavs are now free. The Oder-Neisse line denotes progress. I could also say that the Ashkenazi, European, diaspora has become a world diaspora. That too is progress."

His faith in God forced Maybaum into a less admirable faith in progress and resulted in considerable political naiveté as well as excessive disdain for Orthodoxy. But then, the biblical prophets may also have seemed naive to their contemporaries and they were known to exaggerate in order to make a point.

An aspect of Maybaum's naiveté is his basic lack of appreciation of Jewish sovereignty as reflected in the existence of the state of Israel. Whereas Jewish nationalists have occasionally been tempted to equate post-holocaust progress with the establishment of the state of Israel, Maybaum sees that progress despite Jewish nationalism, not through it. His Judaism is God-centered not land-centered. His interest in Israel arises out of the fact that millions of Jews live there, not because of the political and cultural implications of statehood. The Viennese Jew Ignaz Maybaum was greatly impressed by his only visit to the Jewish state, but the liberal rabbi Ignaz Maybaum was also greatly disturbed by the two poles of secularism and Orthodoxy which he identified with the old pre-holocaust order of things. Somehow, Israel did not quite fit into his notion of *churban* that leads to progress whereas the diaspora did.

The last sermon in his collection *The Faith of the Jewish Diaspora* (London, 1962) sums up his attitude: "The state of Israel is one of the various settlements of the Jewish world diaspora. We see today that the Jewish people remains what it was for two thousand years: a people of the diaspora, a people denied the unity which political and national cohesion gives to the Gentiles. God wills it, and say you all: 'So be it.'" In line with his exaltation of the Jewish home as the center of Jewish life, Maybaum was cautious about the state, any state, including the Jewish state. He called his last book, published posthumously, *Happiness Outside the State* (London, 1980).

What for Emil Fackenheim, and many with him, is a new departure—the holocaust as something *sui generis* in Jewish history; Jewish statehood as a manifestation of radical change in the Jewish condition—is for Maybaum merely a confirmation "that the Jewish people remains what it was for two thousand years," still confined to the trust of Abraham—the *Akeda,* the binding of the biblical Isaac by his father, is a central theme in Maybaum's writings—and the patience of Job. Jewish history, shaped by trust and patience, is the history of progress toward a messianic future. Triumph and tragedy alike are tools in God's hands; the holocaust is no exception.

III

Steven T. Katz is almost outraged by the implications of the idea that the holocaust can be viewed as a sign of progress. He writes that "if the holocaust is the price of freedom, or in this case progress and expiation, then better to do without such evolution and reconciliation—the price is just too high. It is morally and theologically unacceptable. To insist on it is to turn God, *kivyachol* ('as if one could say this'), into a moral monster."

Katz's critique must be taken seriously: "An impossible irony also discloses itself as a corollary of Maybaum's suggestion that God used Hitler for his purposes. If the *Sho'ah* is God's will, if Hitler is 'my servant,' then to resist Hitler is to resist God; to fight the Nazis is to fight the Lord. As such the Warsaw ghetto resisters, the inmates who rebelled at Treblinka, the 'righteous of the nations' who risked death, and more often than not died, to save Jewish lives, all these were rebels against the Almighty."

Katz describes Maybaum as "a victim of his inheritance; that is, of those earlier modernizing attempts which sought to evaluate and interpret Judaism primarily through alien standards and for largely apologetic purposes." He sees too close a connection between Maybaum's *churban* and the crucifixion and assumes that it comes "from Maybaum's great mentor Franz Rosenzweig." This, however, "does not make it true; it merely makes it an error with a pedigree."

The establishment of the state of Israel is seen by Katz as "the antithesis of the crucifixion mentality." He understands the Jewish state to be the mouthpiece of Jews who "have now declared (seemingly with God's permission): we have suffered enough, died enough, been put upon enough; we wish to reject forever our state of powerlessness."

IV

The view that the state of Israel is a sign that the Jewish people has emerged from powerlessness is nowadays commonly held by Jewish historians and theologians alike. On the face of it, it stands as a refutation, perhaps even a condemnation, of Maybaum's position. Had he been a Zionist, he could have used Jewish statehood as "evidence" for his theory; now, however, he has to reject it in favor of a worldwide diaspora. Yet, it seems that some contemporary Jewish thinkers are not too far removed from Maybaum's position although their language and frame of reference are very different. There is a sense of renewal after the holocaust without the rejection of Orthodoxy or Israel, and without a naive affirmation of Western culture and Western diaspora Jewry.

Irving Greenberg is a case in point. Although he shares the view that the holocaust and the state of Israel are signs that Jewish history has entered a new, third, epoch, his description of the two earlier ones shows similarities with Maybaum's understanding of *churban*. In an important essay on the subject, published in 1981 by the National Jewish Resource Center in New York, Greenberg sees the first epoch as the biblical age, "the event . . . of great redemption, the exodus," and the second as the rabbinic age, "an event of great tragedy, the destruction of the temple." He sees the new, third, epoch as a synthesis, "beginning under the sign of a great event of destruction, the holocaust, and a great event of redemption, the rebirth of the state of Israel."

Greenberg hails this new era as something positive and refuses to make a break between what has been—two thousand years of powerless diaspora existence—and what is now: less than four decades of Jewish sovereignty: "Exercise of power must be accompanied by strong models and constant evocation of the memory of historic Jewish suffering and powerlessness. It is so easy to forget slavery's lessons once one is given power, but such forgetfulness leads to the unfeeling affliction of pain on others. . . . Memory is the key to morality."

Echoes of Maybaum's stance are also discernible in Greenberg's understanding of revelation in this new epoch of Jewish history. Daringly Greenberg suggests that the holocaust could be understood as a sign that God has abrogated the covenant with Israel—a thought, incidentally, that Christian missionaries might be tempted, for no good reason, to use for their own purposes. In an essay published by his Center in 1982, Greenberg asserts that, despite God's action, Jews continue to keep the covenant: "But the overwhelming majority of survivors, far from yielding to despair, rebuilt Jewish life and took part in the assumption of power by the Jewish people. . . . Was there ever faith like this faith?" The faith of the saving remnant?

"What then happened to the covenant?" asks Greenberg,

and he offers this answer: "I submit that its authority was broken but the Jewish people, released from its obligations, chose voluntarily to take it on again. We are living in the age of the renewal of the covenant. God was no longer in a position to command, but the Jewish people were so in love with the dream of redemption that it volunteered to carry on its mission." In this way the covenant has remained "a commitment, out of faith, to achieve a final perfection of being." Is the new, voluntary, covenant consistent with the traditional Orthodox position as reflected in the codes of Jewish law, or was Maybaum right after all?

V

Maybaum died without ever reading Irving Greenberg. It is, therefore, impossible to speculate whether he would have seen any points of contact between the views of this Orthodox non-conformist and his own "error with a pedigree." But we are entitled to think of Maybaum as we marvel at the way in which the Jewish people has "picked up the pieces" after the destruction, even to the extent of tempting some of its enemies to assert, despite incontrovertible evidence to the contrary, that the holocaust never happened. We are entitled to reflect, albeit very tentatively—with all of Katz's strictures in mind—whether the tragedy of the holocaust has not opened up new possibilities for the Jewish people by asserting both the continuity with earlier history and the departure from it, which it may one day be legitimate to describe as progress. What Maybaum surmised, Jewish history may vindicate.

Whether that progress will come through Western civilization, in which Maybaum had all too few doubts, or in some other way is not for us to say. But to assert our faith in continued growth of Judaism after the holocaust appears to be legitimate, as is the conviction that this has had a considerable and beneficial impact on Christian thought.

William M. Thompson

Jesus' Uniqueness:
A Kenotic Approach

Gregory Baum and I have often probed the important issue of Jesus' uniqueness together. My consciousness of the problems connected with this belief was emerging while I was pursuing doctoral studies under Dr. Baum's guidance. He once told me that our ecumenical praxis in this area was ahead of our theory, and I would like to try to bring the theory somewhat closer to the praxis in this paper. I know that this issue is close to Dr. Baum's concerns—it surfaces especially in his grappling with the Jewish-Christian complex of problems—and so I hope that this little piece might be a fitting birthday tribute to one of my great teachers.

1. SOME QUESTIONS POSED BY THREE BASIC SOURCES OF CONTEMPORARY THEOLOGY

Broadly speaking, I with many others would consider theology to be a complex, hermeneutical endeavor of correlating the Christian tradition with the concerns of contemporary experience. This two-way hermeneutics involves a willingness to stand under the judgment of both tradition and experience, allowing both to fuse in such a way that one's horizon and praxis is thereby widened and deepened. It is a genuine, not a counterfeit, conversation between past and present that is our aim, rooted in the trust that the God who spoke of old still speaks today within the fabric of our experience without self-contradiction. Now it would seem that three basic sources of our present experience lead us to query anew the tradition of Jesus' uniqueness.

The "voice" of traditional Christianity clearly considers Jesus to be special in some real sense. This is evident from the Greek Scriptures, which give the varied titles of Messiah, Lord, and even God only to Jesus. Paul even speaks of Jesus as inaugurating the "fullness of time" (Gal 4:4), and Hebrews views him as the only and sinless mediator of divine salvation (Heb 4:15; 7:24–25; 10:12–13, etc.). John carries this furthest when he teaches that "no one comes to the Father but through me" (Jn 14:6; cf. 15:4, 6). Clearly, too, the ecumenical Council of Chalcedon was pointing to the specialness of Jesus when it locked horns with Nestorius over the issue of whether Jesus' union with the Divine could be likened to every creature's "moral" union with the Divine through grace. There can simply be no doubt that the specialness of Jesus is a deeply rooted aspect of our Christian heritage, anchored in the precious belief that what occurred in him is of universal and saving significance for all humanity.

And yet the pressures of our contemporary experience are forcing us to query this belief anew. Partly the vigorous theoretical recovery by phenomenological theologians (Blondel, Von Hügel, Rahner, Voegelin, etc.) of the religious depths of our own human interiority has enabled us to believe anew in the divine dimension of every human being. In Rahner's abbreviated formula, every human is an openness to and partial embodiment of the Transcendent. In some sense this means that all of us are divine-human unities, "theandric" in our very self-constitution. At the very least this makes us query the possible differences between Jesus and ourselves, perhaps causing us to wonder whether we might have exaggerated the "Jesus-difference" in Christianity. We are reappropriating anew Paul's realization: "The life I live now is not my own; Christ is living in me" (Gal 2:20). As Voegelin puts it, we need to come to terms with the Christ "in a Babylonian hymn, or a Taoist speculation, or a Platonic dialogue, just as much as in a Gospel." And, as he adds, we cannot "let revelation begin with the Israelite and Christian experiences, when the mystery of divine presence in reality is attested as experienced by man, as far back as ca. 20,000 B.C., by the petroglyphic symbols of the Palaeolithicum."[1]

Linked with this theoretical recovery of the religious depths of human experience is a greater attentiveness to praxis (experience in its practical mode), especially on the part of political theologians. What this means for the specialness of Jesus takes several question-like forms for us. On a rather direct level it makes us ask what is the practical punch of the Jesus event, if Jesus is so qualitatively different from the rest of us. If we cannot model forth in some analogous but real way the life he lived, then why bother to profess belief in him? By making him into a kind of metaphysical exception in human history, are we robbing him of his salvific power to chart and empower a path for the rest of us to pursue? On a larger level, practical theologians have queried some of the possible, more pragmatic consequences of the claims made for Jesus in the Christian past. Is there a link between believing in Jesus' specialness and Christian arrogance and intolerance of outsiders, even persecution of them? Have some forms of Christian specialness provided an ideology for the Constantinian empire and its medieval continuation in Christendom, for anti-semitism and the horrible holocaust, for the denigration of the riches of the world's religions, etc.? Does Christian specialness forever block the ability of Christians to recognize the possible worth *coram Deo* of others in history? These are terribly complex waters; there is no simple correlation between beliefs and behavior through the ages. Yet it is a sound principle to argue that belief and praxis co-condition one another. At the very least the sad history of Christian praxis forces us to probe just what it is we are held to when we profess belief in Jesus' specialness.

A third contemporary dimension of our experience is the relatively new "ecumenic" or "global" horizon of modern humanity. Humanity is surely struggling over the issue of how to live amicably in a complex, interdependent world. Thus far, it would appear that we have not found the correct formula, as the two world wars, the energy crisis, economic instability, and demands for betterment from the third and fourth worlds make painfully evident. We are still in an era of profound struggle, searching for a way to preserve the blessings of particularity, but within a new, more global formula of solidarity. Certainly this raises the issue of how Christianity might contribute to the forging of this global accommodation. Do our claims forever lock us in a stance of Western Christian superiority over others in the world, or are there rich resources within a Jesus-centered tradition which might offer us a via toward a more globally respectful humanity?

A concomitant effect of our slow globalization is the widening of the Christian consciousness beyond Christian frontiers. The new dialogue partners with Christian theology are Hinduism, Buddhism, the religions of the oral cultures, and Judaism, not to mention the archaic religions (a truly global theology must be attentive to the past too). Let me mention the Christian-Buddhist scholar Paul Knitter as an exemplification of this widening of Christian awareness. Without exaggeration, and with a feel for Christian sensitivities, Knitter lays hold of some of the apparent commonalities between Jesus and Buddha which force us to look anew at Jesus' specialness. "The mission of both consisted basically in *revealing* something and in *modeling* what was revealed," he tells us.[2] Both preached an urgent message of liberation (Jesus—the Gospel; Buddha—the Dharma). Both found recognition of their *exousia*/power which flowed from their extraordinary religious experience (Buddha—Nirvana; Jesus—Abba). Both embodied the reality of their revelation: Buddha was called the *Tathagata,* "He who has arrived"; Jesus was called the Messiah. Both likewise were animated by the universality of their message. The Buddhist scholar Richard Drummond claims that Buddhism's sense of universal mission "has no parallel in the previous history of India."[3] Even the content of their messages seems similar: Jesus preaches conversion from lovelessness and injustice; Buddha preaches the call to transcend the ego toward universal compassion. Finally, just as Christianity came to an awareness of Jesus' divine depth only gradually, so too the Mahayanist tradition gradually developed "the nearly complete deification of the Buddha." Knitter adds: "Intrinsic to this interpretation is what Amore terms 'an ancient, legendary pattern' of descent—the Ultimate descends to humanity to become part of it."[4]

2. THE INADEQUACY OF EXCLUSIVITY AND RELATIVISM FOR MANY

Most of us working within the hermeneutical model of theology sketched above would seem to have rejected two previous models put forward on our question. But for comparative reasons, let me briefly sketch their chief tenets. On the one extreme we have what many refer to as the model of exclusivity, which maintains that the divine and liberating work is solely confined to the Jesus event. True liberation is found only in Jesus, nowhere else. Sometimes this model will employ the distinction between prophetic/revealed religions and so-called natural religions, arguing that divine salvation is found only among the first (Judaism by way of anticipation, Christianity now); the latter are only human-made aspirations for the Divine, human shadows of the former. The distinction between the sacred and the profane might also be employed. Space is made, of course, for the exceptional individual who might rise above his or her cultural and religious inheritance and achieve a kind of "implicit" faith, but the religions of the non-Christian orbit are godless in the supernatural sense.

The difficulty for the hermeneutical theologian is that exclusivity lands us in hopeless contradictions on the level of theory, and promotes deleterious practical consequences. Christianity believes in a truly transcendent God whose "sun rises" on all (Mt 5:45). The distinction between a divine-originating and a human-originating religion breaks down in the face of the universal outreach of the God of Christianity. Furthermore, our growing awareness of the religions beyond the Christian orbit seems to confirm this universal divine presence (cf. Knitter and Voegelin). It is not only the case that isolated individuals seem open to the divine presence, but even whole movements, so that in a true sense we can speak of the revealed character of Buddhism, Hinduism, Taoism, the religions of the oral/archaic cultures, etc. The voice of the tradition and the voice of our present experience both would seem to converge in rejecting this model.

While exclusivity seems to be the model characteristic of the rhetoric of fundamentalists (the "right"), religious relativism seems the peculiar tendency of the "left." Relativism, as I am using the term, surfaces in such statements as: "All religions proclaim the same thing"; "All religions are equally good"; "There are no absolute truths, but only equally time-conditioned insights into truth"; "There is nothing peculiarly special about Jesus," etc. As the appeal of exclusivity in a global age is its supposed clarity, so the appeal of relativism is its supposed openness and freedom. But again the hermeneutical theologian will register dissent. The God disclosed in the Jesus event clearly argues against relativism: not all forms of supposed religious piety are consistent with the divine justice and love as taught by Jesus. Jesus' own struggles with the reigning orthodoxies of his time are reduced to meaningless squabbles on relativist assumptions. Further, our own experiences warn us that we need to be discriminating about religious claims, for not all claims emanate from an equally sound analysis of human experience. One of the great difficulties of relativism is that it leaves only raw power as an arbitrator between conflicting claims, or else indifference. To quote Dr. Baum:

> If we simply abandon a universal norm, we are unable to detect the power of evil in the human world and unite with others in a common struggle against it. The 'liberal' view of religious pluralism underestimates this power of evil. Yet the gospel is radical: it applies as critique and promise to the whole of human life.[5]

Again it would seem that the voices of tradition and our experience unite in a rejection of relativism.

3. A KENOTIC INTERPRETATION OF JESUS' UNIQUENESS

Currently hermeneutical theologians are struggling to give birth to a third alternative, one chastened by the inadequacies of the above and consistent with tradition and experience. To my knowledge no *tertium quid* has as yet won consensual agreement, but as a possible contribution, let me propose the thesis of complementary and critical uniqueness as a possible avenue of advance. This thesis is, if you will, a hermeneutical intuition, needing to be fleshed out rather carefully. Let me emphasize that I put this forward only as a thesis in need of much further refinement, by theologians and by the Christian body at large. What is at stake here is the central core of our heritage. The aim is not to deny the universal and saving relevance of the Jesus event (against relativism), but to explicate this in such a way that space might be found for the possible universal and saving relevance of other religious traditions (against exclusivity). Other religious inheritances are involved too. They must be a partner with us in testing our thesis!

3.1. Complementary Uniqueness: Avoiding Exclusivity

But let us proceed. First, our thesis argues for complementary uniqueness for each of the religions, for their founders and tenets. The complementary nature of the religions is entailed, I believe, in the Christian belief in a panentheistic and kenotic God who is intimately present throughout the breadth and depth of the cosmos. Because Christians are convinced that the Divine is disclosed within the contours of universal human experience and the cosmos at large, the capacity to accord a measure of validity to all the varied religions is a Christian possibility. It is the commonality of the one God which ultimately undergirds the complementarity of the religions. If you will, the Divine does not work against itself. But the uniqueness of the varied religions also flows from belief in this one God. The uniqueness of the religions, as I use the term, flows from the belief that the Divine has kenotically self-limited itself and disclosed itself within the necessarily limited, cultural forms of the varied religions and their founders. No one religion and no one religious "sage" is identical to others in all respects, simply because of the unique cultural and historical way in which each realizes its responsiveness to the divine presence. Thus, it is ultimately the divine kenosis of self-emptying into the finite, unique, and limited cultural forms manifest within history which undergirds the uniqueness—the specialness—of each of the religions and of individuals within those religions. We should note here that uniqueness follows from the nature of the Divine itself as a kenotic mystery of self-limitation and weddedness to the diverse and limited vessels of human history. In a real sense this approach is a kenoticist[6] reinterpretation of the older, patristic Logos-doctrine. The strength of that tradition was to argue for the universal presence of the Divine (= Logos) and thus the partial validity of all religions. Its weakness was its inability to account positively for the uniqueness of each of them. Both Troeltsch's earlier proposal and Rahner's anonymous Christian proposal share in the strengths and weaknesses of the standard Logos speculation. A kenoticist reinterpretation views the Divine as also committed to the unique elements of each of the religions, thus viewing them positively as reflections of the divine kenosis, rather than negatively as hindrances to an appreciation of the one true God. Whereas the Logos model would argue that the Divine is present partially in all and supremely in Jesus, its kenoticist variant would propose that the Divine is common to all, but always under the form of kenosis and limitation and particularity, even in Jesus.

Now let us try to unravel some of the implicit consequences of our complementary uniqueness model. First, I think it helps us grasp why there are so many striking similarities among the religions (= complementarity), and yet these similarities are wedded to unique, historical, and cultural differences (= uniqueness). The one God of all always appears under the form of historical kenosis, the universal under the form of particularity. Voegelin would speak of a common structure of human experience shared by all the religions, but uniquely differentiated in varying manners. Thus, history of religions scholars will tell us that Hinduism, Buddhism, Taoism, Islam, Judaism, and Christianity all know the Ultimate/Absolute, but each knows this Absolute in uniquely irreducible manners. The undifferentiated All or Nothing of Hinduism, Taoism, and Buddhism is not identical with the highly personal Allah of Islam who calls supremely for obedience, or with the highly personal Father and Abba of the Jewish and Christian orbits. The cosmic numen of the oral and archaic cultures is not identical with the transcendent God of the world religions.

So, too, many religions recognize that the Absolute discloses itself in history through mediators. All the varied religions in some sense recognize this mediatorial nature of revelation, whether the mediator be a person, an historical process, or liturgy, scriptures, fellowship, etc. But again this commonality of the religions is wedded to historical particularity. There are unique differences between the divine Buddha of the Mahayana who realizes nirvana, the Hindu avatars (Vishnu, Krishna, etc.) who are incarnations of Brahman, and the divine-human Jesus of Christianity who takes the form of solidarity with the oppressed in history. We could extend this partial listing further, but the point has been sufficiently served if we have highlighted the complementary yet unique particularities among the religions.

Second, our model would seem to avoid the well known problems entailed in other views of religions.[7] It would seem more adequate than the notion of a "common essence" or "common core" shared by the religions, because it recognizes that such a common core is actually a reified abstraction which does not exist in the concrete, overlooking the diverse and kenotic forms which the divine liberating activity takes in history. The common core thesis (this is the legacy of the Logos model) overlooks and sometimes denigrates historical and cultural particularity. In the hands of some (viz., Radhakrishnan, Toynbee) it promotes the supposed ecumenical goal of a sort of meta-religion which has distilled this common core to the fullest extent. A variant of the common core model is the "inner-outer" model, which distinguishes between the inner, spiritual core of the religions and their outer liturgical and doctrinal husks. Again, we have a reified abstraction which overlooks historical particularity (that is, kenosis).

Third, our thesis undermines neither the decisiveness (= universal significance) of the Jesus event nor the possible decisiveness of other religious paths. Pointing this out has been Howard Burkle's important contribution to our problem. In a highly suggestive study he argues that the complementarity of the religions "does not destroy the decisiveness of Christianity." Christians can still affirm that their religion, centered on Jesus, makes an essential contribution to humanity's salvation. "For one thing, it is through Jesus that God redeems that segment of humanity who are Christian." Additionally, Christianity offers elements, even to those beyond the Christian orbit, "which certain human beings need, find congenial, and can obtain from no other religion." But moving to the deepest level, Burkle affirms, as would I, that what happened and happens in Jesus is "absolutely decisive for the whole world." If you will, the Jesus event is of salvific import for all of humanity. Burkle thinks that some writers overlook this:

> What is often overlooked about the Christian salvation events is the power of their objectivity. What God has done in Jesus has been *done* and, whether it is accepted or not, it has consequences. God *has* become one with humanity and understood us from within. God *has* suffered with us and forgiven us. God *has* conquered death and sin. And because these things happened in a human life, they are not just concealed within the privacy of God's heart but live on as a part of human history.

But what needs simultaneous affirmation is the possible decisiveness of the other religions:

> What I have been saying about Christianity's decisiveness for others may have a converse. It may be as necessary for Christians to hear of Gautama as it is for Buddhists to hear of Jesus. Gautama's enlightenment at the Bo-tree may also be a salvation event for all people. Perhaps no Christian's salvation is complete until she/he breaks through the wall of the ego, extinguishes wrong desires, and attains that detachment from the world which gives peace. It is possible that the salvation event called Gautama Buddha influences the consciousness of Christians far more profoundly than they realize.[8]

A further implication of our model is that it undermines neither the self-identity of the varied religions nor their possible missionary thrust. It remains the summons of the religions to value and witness to the unique but complementary disclosures of divine revelation that are their basis. To surrender this conviction would be to surrender the unique decisiveness (= universal significance) that each represents. But correspondingly, "conversion" as the traditional goal of missionary witness requires a wider, more global perspective. As we shall see, there is still room for speaking of conversion in the negative sense of "giving up" error and sin. But what our thesis calls for is the notion of conversion as also a "widening" or "expanding": not necessarily a shift from one religion to another, but a widening of one's own religious horizon through openness to the possible wealth found in other religious perspectives. Rather than forfeiting one's religion, perhaps in our global age conversion will increasingly take the form of expanding one's religion. Thomas Merton, perhaps Gandhi, John Dunne and William Johnston come to mind in this regard.

A final implication of our thesis is that it would seem to correspond to our experience, thus permitting an experiential verification of our reinterpretation of the tradition. Our own experience seems to teach us that complementarity and uniqueness can bear a direct rather than inverse relation to one another. Often it is through the mutual enrichment of our relationships with one another that we discover and refine our unique potential. Others complement us in various respects, and, rather than robbing us of our potential, stimulate and catalyze it, helping us to carve out our unique identities. Complementarity and uniqueness can advance together in our autobiographies. So, too, I am suggesting that the same holds true in our collective and even global autobiographies, and this may be the "formula" our global age is struggling to implement strategically. Perhaps the contribution of the venerable religious traditions will be to show how this is possible theologically and practically.

In theological terms, I would suggest that the mutual complementarity that we experience in life is a reflection of the creative and salvific God who grounds our human commonality. Likewise, our discovery of uniqueness reflects the divine kenosis which uniquely summons each of us into being and self-limits itself in such a way that our unique potential and freedom can thrive. Just as the God of complementarity and uniqueness does

not work against himself, just as complementarity and uniqueness can thrive harmoniously in our own lives; so can they thrive
together on the global level of the religions and humanity at large.

3.2. The Critical Dimension: Avoiding Relativism

If the first "horn" of our thesis attempts to avoid exclusivity,
this second "horn" seeks to avoid relativism. At least in principle
I would not maintain that all religions are necessarily equal in all
respects, representing equally adequate expressions of humanity's religious experience. Religions can be complementary without necessarily being equally adequate. This is true within our
personal experience, and there seems no compelling reason to
doubt its truth on the global level. I suppose that this is a part of
the kenotic mystery of history: the Divine is wedded to our boils
and cataracts too!

Thus, for example, all religions are tempted by sin and self-
idolatry, all are to some extent uniquely wedded to limited cultural perspectives, etc. Religions (and their founders) represent
an intersection of the Divine and human—an intersection is not
a simple identification. A few more examples may help. Typically, religions of the oral cultures, while highlighting the divine
presence within the cosmos, fail to recognize that the Absolute
also transcends nature. Turning it around, a typical danger of
transcendent religions is dualism: a denigration of the cosmos,
overshadowing divine immanence with transcendence. Islam's
holy war ideology would seem defective in Christian eyes when
measured against Jesus' God of love. Judaism's stress on the cov-
enantal nature of religion is a corrective to simply individualistic
forms of piety. Buddhism's mystical nirvana can correct religions
which ignore the mystical dimension of religion. Jesus' more
active stress on solidarity with the oppressed challenges the social
lethargy of some religions. In short, religions know inadequacies
and are in need of correction. Our desire to be responsive to the
world's religions need not make us naive.

The same critical sensitivity holds for individuals within the
varied religions too. Complementary uniqueness is just that:
complementarity, not equality and identity. We need not hold

that all individuals are equal in the way in which they body forth
the divine presence. Christians can surely maintain that Jesus
uniquely and consummately bodies forth the divine presence in
his life, death, and resurrection in a way that no one else does.
Christians surely know from their own experience of sinful infi-
delity, not to mention their own unique histories, that there is
not a simple relation of identity or equality between themselves
and Jesus. Complementarity, yes; identity and equality, no. So,
too, there are no texts which would lead us to believe that Jesus
is simply equal with or identical to any other religious sage of
history. To pursue another example, Buddha's own unique realization of nirvana is his own unique and decisive breakthrough.
A critical use of our complementary uniqueness pattern does not
land us in untenable views about equality and identity.[9]

4. POSTSCRIPT

Does this approach do full justice to what Christians have
traditionally affirmed about Jesus? At this point I think we must
say that the Scriptures are somewhat ambiguous in this regard.
To my knowledge no biblical scholar has as yet thoroughly studied this issue. My own tentative view would be that the deepest
thrust of the New Testament avoids both exclusivity and relativism. It is a major thrust of Jesus' proclamation that God is universally available (against exclusivity), as well as critical of injustice and lovelessness (against relativism). Further, kenoticism is
a deep strand of the New Testament (cf. Phil 2:7), and we have
done little more than draw out some of its relevant applications
to our theme. It would seem to make sense to interpret the Scriptures against the backdrop of this kenotic, non-exclusive, non-
relative horizon. If some texts appear to be exclusivistic (viz.,
Heb 4:7, 10; Jn 14:6; 15:4, 6), perhaps we can ascribe this to their
limited theological and cultural horizon. Most of the biblical
texts, and even Chalcedon, can be read as proclaiming the unique
decisiveness for salvation of Jesus.

Should we go further and maintain that Jesus is the highest
mediator of salvation? It is not unambiguously clear that this is

the scriptural teaching. Perhaps Paul's famous text about Jesus as initiating the "fullness of time" (*pleroma;* Gal 4:4) can be so read, but I would suggest that this text needs to be read in the light of the kenoticism which is such a deep feature of Paul's theology. It is a kenotic fullness which has come in Jesus: the Ultimate has decisively appeared and saved humanity, but under the form of kenosis and self-limitation, subject to the partial and fragmentary limits of human history. Thus, as Rosemary Ruether likes to say, we still await the second coming. The eschatological breakthrough of Jesus remains proleptic and incomplete. Under kenoticist presuppositions it is possible to say that the Highest/the Absolute has arrived, but we must add: under the form of kenosis. I would suggest that the tradition has been rightly fascinated by the first element of the affirmation: the Highest has come. But the kenoticist proviso has generally been either suppressed by the tradition or remained subterranean: under the form of kenosis.[10]

Let me end by suggesting a speculative thought. The current and painful globalization through which we are passing is enormously difficult. In Christian terms it is a living out of the death-resurrection mystery on a global scale; in Jewish terms, a global exodus; in Buddhist, a global nirvana. Such a process is finally a global experience of transcendence (one of the great signals of transcendence of our times) which requires the ultimately Transcendent One to ground and sustain it. Perhaps a Transcendence self-limited to kenosis, a kenotic Logos, affords us an analogous model of what our holy God is up to. For only the truly Transcendent could globally unify in solidarity the race and cosmos, but only a Kenotic One could do so in such a way that our unique particularities are not destroyed in the process.

NOTES

1. Eric Voegelin, "Response to Professor Altizer's 'A New History and a New But Ancient God?'" *Journal of the American Academy of Religion,* 43 (1975), 766, 767.

2. Paul F. Knitter, "Horizons on Christianity's New Dialogue with Buddhism," *Horizons,* 8 (1981), 56–58.

3. Richard H. Drummond, *Gautama the Buddha: An Essay in Religious Understanding* (Grand Rapids: Eerdmans, 1974), p. 44.

4. Knitter, *art. cit.,* 57.

5. In his "Introduction" to Rosemary Radford Ruether, *Faith and Fratricide: The Theological Roots of Anti-Semitism* (New York: Seabury, 1974), p. 15.

6. The most helpful entry into kenoticism is Geddes MacGregor, *He Who Lets Us Be: A Theology of Love* (New York: Seabury, 1975). For the classical Logos approach, see Lucien Richard, *What Are They Saying About Christ and World Religions?* (New York: Paulist, 1981).

7. Cf. Howard R. Burkle, "Jesus Christ and Religious Pluralism," *Journal of Ecumenical Studies,* 16 (1979), 467–469, for an overview and bibliography.

8. *Ibid.,* 464–466.

9. People often confuse equality of potentiality with equality of actualization. The second is what I argue against.

10. The peculiar logic of kenoticist thought allows a both/and mode of discourse, rather than an either/or: the Highest has appeared, but within human limits; unchangeable, but freely changing, etc.

Philip McKenna

Psychoanalysis and Socialism in Conflict

In 1970, Gregory Baum published an article in *The Ecumenist* (VIII, 5, pp. 72–75) titled "Prospective Theology" in which he outlined a theological method different from "normative theology." Whereas normative theology "focuses on God's self-communication in Israel and Jesus Christ as handed on by the Church, and therefore looks to the normative revelations of the past," prospective theology "is the discernment of, and the systematic reflection on, God's ongoing self-communication in history and the cosmos" (*ibid.,* p. 73).

In the past, theology has been in dialogue mainly with philosophy, but Baum's work has increasingly been a prospective theology concentrated on a theological reading of psychology and sociology. *Man Becoming* (1970) gave us his theological exploration using predominantly psychological categories, and after his two years at the New School of Social Research in New York (1969–71), he wrote *Religion and Alienation: A Theological Reading of Sociology* (1975).

Baum's shift to socio-political analysis is not merely a case of this after that, but marks a theoretically preferred emphasis. He argues that "anxiety and neurosis" are to be "understood largely in social and political terms" (1982, p. 92), though this is in an article attempting to retrieve subjectivity in a socially responsible psychotherapy.

Baum has argued in a workshop (1985) that (1) there is a place for both political analysis/praxis and therapeutic analysis/praxis, (2) that attempts to reduce one to the other are misplaced, and (3) that the contradictions between the two should not be glossed over or thought to be easily resolved. This requires a dialectical equanimity rare in human life and almost totally absent from our Western intellectual traditions.

In the spirit of that intellectual virtue, I thought it might be useful to highlight some areas of conflict between these two ways of understanding and transforming human life. For clarity's sake and because I think it the most potentially fruitful dialogue, I will restrict myself to the conflict between psychoanalysis and a broadly Left politics.

INDIVIDUALISM

Psychoanalysis is theoretically and, especially practically, an essentially individualistic enterprise. Herein it is unreflectively the heir of Reformation pietism and the secular Enlightenment preoccupation with individual consciousness. Its starting point is the monad of individual consciousness. That it considers this a viable starting point and object of therapy means that it tends to abstract from social realities. This has consequences. First, it remains blind to the essentially social definition of human beings. Think how inconceivable human consciousness is without the possession of an actual language, and how that language is the distilled influence of countless other generations in an evolving form of social order. Second, because this inherence of culture and society in the very essence of the individual is largely ignored, the social order within which I perceive myself as disturbed and so do my therapy is statically accepted as the reality which teaches me my limitations and to which I have to adjust. Or, if my aim is not consciously adjustment but a kind of personal integration of my unruly instincts, the given social order is assumed to be the place where that is possible if only I do all the individual things necessary for personal liberation. This world which is rich enough and stable enough to allow me a major concentration of energy on personal liberation and happiness is not the world of the exhausted poor, the starving, the colonized, the tortured, the imprisoned. It is the world of the economically and politically comfortable.

Where it does deal with social relationships, psychoanalysis tends not to go beyond the individual's sexual relationships and his or her nuclear family. Two observations about this. First, there is the practical implication that these are the truly significant and influential relationships for the individual with respect to both the formation and the resolution of emotional disturbances. Economic relationships, cultural definition, gender, and the history of one's race, people, or nation seem less relevant or disappear entirely from consideration. Second, even in its treatment of interpersonal relationships, psychoanalysis is so influenced by the solipsistic individualism of the secular Enlightenment tradition that relations with others are called "object" relations. In that tradition, the polarity is between subject and object. Object is anything not the subject. The object of the subject may be personal or not. Even its extra-psychic existence is not assumed but laboriously established. While it is true that Freud's avoidance of philosophy and his biological emphasis free him from excesses in this direction (so that he reads generally more like an Aristotelian), his acceptance of the isolated individual and his consciousness as the starting point pulls him toward the post-Cartesian ignorance of the fact that persons are socially created and defined. The other is an object, and the love of the other is not a given, but must be explained by an elaborate logic of self-gratification.

If psychoanalysis gets into trouble by abstraction of individuals from their social definition, political analysis is prone to the reverse error through abstraction *from* the individual. It tends to analyze human beings in groups, races, religions, nations, classes, genders, parties, institutions, movements and isms. It conceives these as agents and patients in history. It is, therefore, more abstract than therapeutic analysis which, in practice, is held to the uniqueness of individuals. In general, the more abstract an analysis, the more vulnerable it is to illusions. Its unities are often granfalloons with significant existence only in minds or, more dangerously, in many like minds.

Therapy of the individual highlights or brings to consciousness the personal sources of illusion in that blind adhesion to leaders, groups, or causes which can be seen to be a major cause of the infliction of horrors upon other human beings.

Socialist analysis saw in Western individualism the ideological self-interest of an economically dominant class. Its targets were philosophical individualism and laissez-faire capitalism, and its offensive arguments were prepared well before the arrival on the cultural scene of the new complexities of depth psychology. The baby was thrown out with some very dirty bathwater. First, there was such a concentrated emphasis on the economic realities as determinative of the course of history that even human culture, let alone the spiritual life of individuals, was treated with a fierce reductionism that has been under correction only in recent socialist theory. Second, there was the pressure to act. Philosophers were seen as seduced to political passivity by being given leisure to think forever. Socialist theory was not just another theory but a call to change the world politically in place of merely understanding it. From its own logic and because of the repressive reaction of the dominant capitalist societies, a long war was begun. The first casualty is truth, and the second is the value of the individual. In the battle it does not concern the general whether the soldier holds his ground through love, hate or fear. To question is treason. Terror becomes an acceptable political instrument. Totalitarian order becomes "necessary" to control mulish individuals in the struggle to survive. Only weak ideas of a glorious future make this state of things different from that repression of the poor which was the original enemy.

Christianity with its Gospel principle of self-critique and its history of self-renewal might well be expected to understand why revolutions repeat that destruction of individuals against which the revolutions are mounted in the first place. But Christianity stood historically as the enemy and with the enemy, and in its efforts to extricate and renew itself, it has signally failed in two crucial areas. Since the Constantinian crossroad, it has remained blind to the demonic in its economic and political power. And, second, where we might expect a search for wisdom about human sexuality, we find a rigid reliance on the pseudo-clarity of law.

Psychoanalysis puts the burden on the individual to explore with the new language of the unconscious the roots of actions which may seem to be one thing and then turn out to be another.

The person who seeks power for consciously good ends may come to know that what drives him or her is fear and hatred of the mother. The theorist of utopian hopes may find he or she is engaged in building an elaborate web of illusion to cover and deny the flight from bodily existence and the despair of attaining sexual happiness. The person warmed by adhesion to a noble cause may find within an insatiable paranoia that needs an enemy. Because the individual analyzes himself or herself rather than the social underpinnings, the individual freedom and responsibility for transformation are constantly highlighted.

SELF-TRANSCENDENCE

Therapists, among themselves, sometimes talk about the "curse" of therapy. By this they mean that one can become so enamored with the exploration of one's own unconscious that one is endlessly drawn to the details of one's own past and the feelings one has about them. That we can name this pathological narcissism might seem to relieve us, but the structure of analysis is singularly weak in instruments for dealing with it. One is removed from "real life," the session is totally for the client, moral confrontation is eschewed, the analyst's time is bought, he or she is self-effacing and completely attentive to the thoughts and feelings of the client.

The ability to work and love and perhaps to die well may be the stated goals of therapy, but these seem to be socially imposed (as from without) on a creature of instincts whose aim is gratification. Nothing from our deepest self moves us to the other in love. Love is a hard-won skill forced on the self-serving organism by a parsimonious and frustrating reality.

You can discern here an anthropology that is at least a cousin of the one behind empiricist moral theory and social contract political theory. Its compatibility with consumer capitalism in its North American form is obvious. Commentators have remarked how conformed and without an edge of social criticism they find the world of American analysis. Many European analysts were active socialists, but most of those who emigrated to the United States fell silent for the sake of acceptance as citizens and perhaps for the sake of psychoanalysis.

I describe here not a practical trap that psychoanalysis *must* fall into. Rather in naming the trap itself, psychoanalysis is often able to avoid it. To put it in another way, the analysand often has more going for him or her than narcissistic self-involvement. The theoretical crux I described is another matter altogether, because it remains uncriticized within psychoanalysis, and its connection with the practical trap is not seen. The Lacanian Schneiderman can write approvingly that psychoanalysis has to do with the recovery of desire, and that "the road to desire does not pass through *agape* or *philia* or *caritas*" (Schneiderman, p. 85).

Psychoanalysis, seeing how the call to self-transcendence has so often been from outside the self, an instrument for an institution (e.g., a church) to control people, deny them their desires, and demand impossible sacrifices of them, is rightly suspicious of the language. To be suspicious and to champion the underdog of desire is one thing, but to give no defining place to the human being's ability to love another as oneself and even die for that person leaves psychoanalysis self-blinded and self-limited in a quite unnecessary way.

One concomitant of this narrowed view of the human heart and something that is adduced in evidence for it is the assertion that human hostility and natural aggression are also basic to human nature. They are desire's warriors in a world of scarcity. Humans are held in check only by outside force—actual police and the inner police of superego put there by the outer powerful ones. "Hate, as a relation to objects", said Freud, "is older than love" ("Instincts and Their Vicissitudes," *S.E.,* XIV, 138).

Prospects for human transformation especially on a large scale are very dim in this view, because there is no principle of hope, no grasp of how the power of human self-transcendence in loving could build a world of cooperation without war.

Socialism, trumpeting its hope for humankind's future, calling people to great sacrifice for that future, joining its activists together in supportive groups, is clearly the heir of the originally religious view of humankind as inherently self-transcendent. Many on the left have spoken of enlargement of spirit, the healing of narrowness and rigidity that come from sharing in a political task which often gradually becomes the same thing as sharing lives. They are drawn into comradeship, they are encouraged to open their hearts and minds to people all over the world and in the future, they are trusted to be generous with time and energy.

Also, because these people are allied in a questioning and critical stance toward the values and institutions of their society, they often find the courage to throw off the more excessive or onerous demands of the social superego. So people in radical movements often find access to a bodily and sexual energy hitherto repressed, and they organize their relationships in unconventional ways.

Now the impression one gets from hearing all this is that involvement in a movement of political action actually effects healing and transformation of human beings at the personal level, such as is aimed at in psychoanalytic therapy. Also, it seems to do this indirectly, without the trap of self-involvement, and in a context where the liberated energy immediately has socially transforming consequences.

Too good to be true? Well, there are several points to make parallel to what was said about self-transcendence in psychoanalysis. First, in the area of theory, socialism, heir as was psychoanalysis to the rejection of Christianity, narrowed its definition of human nature to a materialistic base, leaving no logical possibility of including self-transcendence within that definition. This was, however, clearly implicit in socialist praxis and within the exhortation to give all to the cause and love the brothers.

Second, and this is partly a function of the gap between theory and practice, there is a certain quality of transience and inflation to these reported transformations. Socialist groups, for all their intensity and transforming power, seem to fall apart over emotional conflicts that surface more powerfully when the group moves toward more total life commitment. Even if emotional disturbances are predominantly socially caused, socialism has no language for dealing with them in the concrete. It can throw at them only social analysis and general moral exhortation. Here it pays for its abandonment of individuality and the geography of subjectivity.

Compare this with the staying power of religious groups, which have engaged people in their individuality, and at the level of sexuality and family—the locus, after all, for the first emergence of self-transcendence. Potentially disintegrative emotional conflicts here are handled by morality and by encompassing people within community rituals, especially vows and sacraments.

CONCLUSION

Under the two headings of individualism and self-transcendence, I have touched on many areas of conflict between psychoanalysis and socialist politics. Others that could be explored are: the meaning of authority, the origin of morality, and feminism. It must be evident also that I think a religious voice must be a participant in the dialectic. It may even provide a key to some fruitful resolutions in the future.

BIBLIOGRAPHY

Baum, Gregory. *Man Becoming.* New York: Herder and Herder, 1970.
————. *Religion and Alienation, A Theological Reading of Sociology.* New York: Paulist Press, 1975.
————. "Prospective Theology," *The Ecumenist,* VIII, 5 (1970), pp. 72–75.
————. "The Retrieval of Subjectivity," *Canadian Journal of Community Mental Health,* I, 1 (March 1982), pp. 89–102.
Freud, Sigmund. "Instincts and Their Vicissitudes" (1915), in *The Standard Edition of the Complete Psychological Works,* Vol. XIV, pp. 111–140.
Schneiderman, Stuart. *Jacques Lacan—The Death of An Intellectual Hero.* Cambridge, Mass.: Harvard University Press, 1983.

Joe Holland

The Post-Modern Paradigm
Implicit in the Church's
Shift to the Left

INTRODUCTION

In recent times it has been widely noted that the Catholic Church is undergoing a shift to the left. In this essay, I would like to unfold the hypothesis that this shift to the left, while obviously breaking the Church's working alliance with liberalism or capitalism during the twentieth century, implicitly contains both *a post-Marxist and even a post-modern social and religious paradigm.* I would further propose that it contains implicitly the seeds of a new ecumenical Christian theology. (In some future essay, I would like to probe the possibility that this post-modern paradigm actually draws on recessive elements in the socialist tradition, not the dominant "scientific" stream, but rather communitarian, populist, religious, and even utopian variants.)

There is no space in this essay to do more than unfold the hypothesis by contrasting what I propose as the emerging post-modern paradigm with an interpretation of prior modern and classical paradigms, nor am I prepared at this point to do much more. Thus I will not here argue for the truth of this hypothesis, nor chronicle its development in historical events. As such then the hypothesis functions here as an intuitive proposal, what Paul Ricoeur would call a hermeneutical "guess" to guide further work.[1]

It has been often argued that this Catholic shift to the left represents a Catholic surrender to Marxism or to the secular humanism of modernity.[2] But I am suggesting that, while the

39

shift to the left has occurred within the context of a new Catholic encounter with both Marxism and modernity, nonetheless the actual Catholic praxis (if not always the articulated theory) increasingly carries an implicit post-Marxian and even post-modern paradigm, and certainly a post-liberal one.[3]

In proposing this hypothesis, I will first sketch the end of the cultural period called the modern world. Then I will sequentially review the classical Catholic paradigm, the initial modern liberal paradigm, and the Marxian radicalization of the modern paradigm. Next I will sketch the newly emerging post-modern paradigm proposed as implicit in the Catholic Church's shift to the left. Finally, I will conclude with some theological observations about an ecumenical theology rooted in this post-modern paradigm.

THE END OF THE MODERN WORLD

The modern world as a coherent period of social history began roughly in the sixteenth century and is now coming to an end. Prior to the sixteenth century, pre-modern consciousness as fate still dominated the West. This meant a fatalistic acceptance of nature and history in all their limits and tragedies as reflecting God's immutable ordering of the world. Obviously individual giants like empire builders defied fate to change history, but even they saw themselves as the carriers of fate, and represented oppressive fate to those whom they controlled.

There have been many names for this pre-modern period in the life of the West—traditional society, classical society, feudalism, etc. But in the eighteenth century historians agree that a new spirit was taking hold.

This new or modern spirit promised to liberate humanity from fate. It promised to break the religiously legitimated authoritarian constraints of classical Catholic tradition and its institutions. It promised a new vision, centered in secular science, and reaching for freedom and progress for all the world.

Renaissance humanism was midwife to this new cultural world-view, but its birth came forth in the Enlightenment. It was the Enlightenment which promised to unleash the light of reason to shatter all residues of superstition and ignorance. The Enlightenment became the intellectual or cultural foundation for the modern world.[4]

The modern world has unleashed the most productive powers of control over nature and history. Compared to the modern scientific world, all prior history marked but the infancy or even pre-history of humanity. For thousands of years human civilization had wandered in ignorance and superstition, immersed in biological, historical, and above all religious fate. Yet in a few hundred years, the modern world changed everything.

The modern world ushered in a trajectory of ever expanding progress, whereby the wonders of one generation became but the stepping off point of the next. For example, secret mathematical theories of tiny cliques of priests and philosophers in ages past became the simple working tools of millions of elementary and secondary school children. The modern world unleashed technology, politics, economics, and culture from nearly every restraint. So powerful was this modern vision that today it has become the only way most of us can conceive reality.

But in the late twentieth century, the modern vision grows culturally exhausted. This is because its vision of human freedom and progress is now backfiring.

The end result of the modern world is increasingly a new, more powerful and destructive technological fate. The modern world has begun to build a powerful and destructive scientific cage for humanity and nature. Worse than pre-modern fate, this modern fate threatens to destroy the earth and all humanity. Even short of that total destruction, late modern fate has already unleashed great forces of interim destruction.

Only in the twentieth century did the destructive side of modern world become clear. Only in this generation did consciousness of it spread widely across our culture.

The first major expression was World War I, a war of terrible technological ferocity breaking down the distinction between soldier and civilian. But it was justified as a final act, a war to end all war.

Soon came World War II, infinitely more destructive with

the slow saturation and fire bombing of major population centers, and the instantaneous atomic bombing of Japan. Contemplating this fate, Pius XII wrote, "There will be no song of victory, only the inconsolable weeping of humanity, which in desolation will gaze upon the catastrophe brought on by its own folly."

Two other modern abominations rose out of World War II. The first was the scientific extermination of most of European Jewry. The second was the rise from both capitalism and socialism of scientific totalitarian states.

Later other themes of destruction would come before the late modern consciousness. The most powerful recently has been awareness of the slow ecological poisoning of the planet. A still more subtle one has been what might be called the poisoning of humanity's social ecology—the steady erosion of the delicate fabric of family, neighborhood, and community. Of course the overriding factor is the fear of nuclear destruction for nature and humanity.

Meanwhile, in the midst of the greatest technological productivity of all human history, we develop a new consciousness of the poor. They are systematically excluded, in ever larger numbers, precisely by modern scientific civilization.

And beneath this all grows an ever deepening secularization, shutting out the awe and power of the religious mystery.

Thus we see the negative climax of the modern scientific promise of freedom and progress—ever more destructive wars, threats of nuclear annihilation, genocide, totalitarianism, ecological poisoning, the erosion of human community, the marginalization of the poor, and denial of religious mystery.[5]

What emerged in the eighteenth century as a bold dream converts itself dialectically in the late twentieth century into a frightening nightmare. This is the end of the modern world.

Presently two modern scientific ideologies do battle with each other over who shall triumph in this end period. But by so doing, they deepen their mutual path of violence across nature and history. These two ideologies are orthodox liberalism and orthodox Marxism, or scientific capitalism and scientific socialism, typified by the United States and the Soviet Union.

Actually, the two are becoming less alternatives to each other and more sequential expressions of the same dialectical thrust of the Enlightenment. Both are headed on a path of negative and destructive convergence.

Both liberalism and Marxism are ideologies of modern secular freedom and progress. They share common roots in the Enlightenment vision. Yet Marxism has not provided a radical alternative to liberalism, but only a radicalization if it. And liberalism, rather than providing an alternative to the totalitarian expression of Marxism in Soviet communism, is now generating a parallel and convergent totalitarianism of its own. This is the modern crisis—not of one ideology, but of both modern ideologies.

At the foundation of both ideologies is the common root metaphor of the machine as the cultural image of nature and humanity. (I am indebted to Gibson Winter for highlighting how this metaphor of the machine came to function at that foundation of the cultural imagination of the modern period.[6] It is a machine, however, which is increasingly turning against humanity and nature.

THE CLASSICAL LEGACY

Before examining the liberal and Marxian ideologies, it might be helpful to review how the *pre-modern classical Catholic world view* perceived these elements.

Ideologies, or more broadly world-views, can be examined in terms of their interpretation of the following elements: (1) history; (2) structure; (3) religion; (4) governance; (5) root metaphor. Thus one might review the classical legacy as follows.

(1) *History:* The future was seen as continuation of the past, that is, history was a broad repetitive cycle of biological birth and decay, but with a non-historical cosmic core of eternal truth providing the transcendent "soul" of the civilization, protected by rock-like institutions. This combination of fortress and transcendence provided the foundation for the symbiosis of uprooted metaphysics and arrogant imperialism which typified the classi-

cal West. That fortified transcendence was seen as an escape from nature and biology. It provided the foundation for a dualistic disparaging of creation.

(2) *Structure:* Hierarchical order was the basic structure with material regeneration marking the lowest regions and sexless transcendent spirituality the highest ones. Hierarchy was the key structural principle and the lower existed for the higher.

(3) *Religion:* In this non-historical hierarchical view, all reality emanated from and returned to the divine source as in a chain of being. All reality was thus religious, though biological life was remote from the divine. Religion was the transcendent control point, fortified in stable heavy institutions.

(4) *Governance:* The system was hierarchically ruled from the top down, in order to protect the tradition (history), preserve the order (structure), and guarantee the institutions (eternal core). Rule had a religious character.

(5) *Root Metaphor:* Externally the basic principle of imagination was biological. Nature and society were modeled on Aristotelian biology. But internally this was supplemented by a combination of high spiritual transcendence (the soul of the civilization) encased in rock-like institutions (immune from biological cycle of birth and decay and witnessed to by the exclusion of sexuality from the sanctuary). The root metaphor was thus a dualism of body and soul.

Thus the pre-modern or classical Catholic vision was one of tradition, fixed order, hierarchical rule, unchanging institutions, total sacralism, and a combination of the biological organic metaphor with the transcendent soul encased in a military fortress. This was the vision of Christian civilization, or Christendom.[7]

A visual illustration of the world-view can be seen in Figure A.

THE MODERN CHALLENGE FROM LIBERALISM

The first challenge to this pre-modern Catholic world view came from the ideology of liberalism.[8] The pattern of its worldview is as follows:

(1) *History:* It unleashed the future (progress) in an evolu-

Figure A—The Classical Catholic Vision

History as static cycle of birth and decay. (Tradition)

Structure as hierarchical rock-like institutions of civilization (Order)

Transcendent　spiritual　core　of　eternal　truth (Contemplation)

Root metaphor: Body as organic and soul as transcendent spirit protected by rock-like fortress against biological decay tionary trajectory by breaking the hold of the past. This was a dualistic temporal axis of evolutionary modernization versus traditional stasis.

(2) *Structure:* Liberalism shattered the former order of the hierarchical whole to maximize the autonomy of the parts (atomistic freedom) in the whirling competition of economics (free market), politics (interest groups) and culture (free thought).

(3) *Religion:* There has been a progressive privatization and marginalization of religious energies in order to guarantee the autonomy of the self and the secular, advanced by science and technology. Science became the religion of the public realm, while individualistic pietism became the religion of the private realm. Both the biological rhythm and the contemplative transcendence of the classical pattern were dissolved into the linear drive of the machine for production (activism).

(4) *Governance:* The mode of rule passed into management, which tried to respect the autonomy of the parts (pluralism) and yet avoid the dual extremes of no order (anarchism) or tyranny (hierarchy). This was expressed by an invisible hand, which in hidden ways brings harmony from the autonomous parts.

(5) *Root Metaphor:* It is the machine of Newtonian physics whose autonomous parts act as counter-pressures to each other and thereby advance the machine's trajectory of production.

This vision became the cultural foundation of industrial capitalism, of liberal democracy, and of liberal culture. It is focused on progress as evolution, freedom as competition, and a dualism of private religiosity and public secularism, all guided by technocratic pragmatism. A visual illustration of this image can be seen in Figure B.

THE RADICALIZATION OF MODERNITY OF MARXISM

The second major challenge to the classical world-view and simultaneously to the liberal one came from Marxism. Yet again Marxism proved not a radical alternative to the liberal Enlightenment vision, but only a radicalization of its foundational principles. For Marxism, liberalism was not scientific enough. Lib-

Figure B—The Modern Liberal Vision

History as linear arrow of progress (Progress)
Structure as fragmentation (Freedom)
Religion as privatized redemption (Pietism or technique)
Root metaphor: Simple machine

eralism opened the door to a scientific society, but had not followed through all the way. This Marxism would do.

By Marxism here I mean what is often referred to as orthodox or scientific Marxism, that is, the form of thought which triumphed in the Soviet state. There is much debate about to what degree Marx himself can be held accountable for this, and how much is independently derived from Engels, Lenin, Stalin, and pre-modern Russian history.[9]

I would propose the position that Marx's thought in this regard has two sides to it, one side advancing the most destructive features of Enlightenment rationality (the scientific positivist side) and the other side straining to reach beyond the limits of the Enlightenment toward a post-modern society (the truly dialectical Hegelian side). But I believe the former became dominant in Marxism, while the latter proves creative only when retrieved in a post-Marxian framework.[10]

Some might ask: What of social democracy, or what has more recently come to be called democratic socialism? Again I have two statements on this. On the one hand, it stands midway between the logic of the liberal and Marxian ideologies, and so suffers from the crisis of each as well as being caught in their negative convergence. On the other hand, since it has some relative independence from both the main lines of liberalism and the main lines of orthodox Marxism, it could provide a creative historical space for probing the post-modern vision, much as is happening in contemporary Catholicism. If that is true, then democratic socialism could provide a seed of the post-Marxist and post-modern vision. But to do that would require a deep internal cultural struggle, for it is still imprisoned in Enlightenment rationality—in its sterile secularism, its uprooted cosmopolitanism, its pro-statist and anti-communitarian drift, in sum its burden of radical modernity.

Marxism directed its critique of liberalism to the massive social injustices of industrial capitalism. In many cases it was able to form an alliance of its left intelligentsia with the victims of modern liberalism, especially with the industrial proletariat and later with the displaced peasantry of the third world.

Marxism's critique of capitalism remains sound, but in the

words of Roberto Mangabeira Unger it is only a partial critique.[11] It hides the more powerful and underlying Marxian drive to further the secular scientific rationalization of society. To understand better that drive, I will unfold basic elements of the orthodox Marxian ideology.

(1) *History:* The future is still unleashed again by breaking with the past, but this time in revolutionary fashion. The arrow of progress does not just gradually evolve, but makes an apocalytic turn upward with revolution. So sharp is the turn that in post-revolutionary Marxism the tendency is to shut out both past and future. The past is shut out as totally corrupt. The future is shut out by creating an eschatological consolidation which is threatened by the subversion of on-going historical consciousness. Thus the Marxian view tends toward two views of history—apocalyptic before the revolution and static after it. Science comes into fulfillment with a socialist state.

(2) *Structure:* The shattered liberal whole is reordered under the guidance of the scientific socialist intelligentsia. Again there are two moments: the pre-revolutionary organization of workers into a mass block in the factory model under the strategic guidance of socialist intellectuals (the party) for the purpose of forcing the capitalist class off the field (a force field analysis from Newtonian physics); and later the scientific reorganization of the whole society by the elites of the scientific state.

(3) *Religion:* The secular/religious dualism of liberalism dissolves into total secularization. Religion is either totally suppressed, or begrudgingly controlled by the state as a temporary concession to residual pre-modern elements. Autonomous secular science, centered in the state, emerges as the modern religion.

(4) *Governance:* Reason or intelligence becomes the direct governing principle, replacing fatalistic hierarchical rule from the pre-modern period, and the elite management of progressive competition in the liberal form. But lacking any truly religious foundation, reason collapses into instrumental rationality where the state becomes the absolute expression of reason. Democracy is "fulfilled" in the manipulative intelligence of the technocratic, or, worse, totalitarian state.

(5) *Root Metaphor:* It is again the machine. But different

from the overtly unguided machine of liberalism, it becomes now a formally intelligent or cybernetic machine. The party and later the state become the formal mind of the social machine. The pre-modern structure of hierarchy and the pre-modern historical condition of fate return.

Thus the ideological vision of Marxism radicalizes liberalism by stressing in the pre-revolutionary moment an apocalyptic turning point (the revolution), mass force or total power, secularization, and scientific politics. In the post-revolutionary phase, however, it reverses back to a new mechanized pre-modern view by stressing stasis and order, and a state invested with an absolute character. The root metaphor remains the machine, but a cybernetic one guided by intelligence—first in the revolutionary intelligentsia, then elite state bureaucrats. (See Figure C.)

TOWARD CAPITALIST TOTALITARIANISM

But this critique of Marxism should be no consolation to the Right, for liberalism is in turn dialectically shifting in its worldview toward the same totalitarian tendency which first surfaced from the Marxian side. I have spelled this out elsewhere as the rise of the national security state.[12]

Liberalism originally represented an under-developed phase of the mechanistic metaphor at the foundation of the modern world. Marxism by contrast represented an early anticipation of its more cybernetic and totally rationalized conclusion. But now that conclusion is upon us and liberalism succumbs with Marxism to total rationalization of instrumental reason and its destructive energies.

Both the liberal and Marxian ideologies can be seen as founded on the mechanics of Newtonian physics. The initial liberal version is that of a machine whose parts are in equilibrium, and thereby proceeding evenly on a progressive trajectory. The Marxian version sees the pre-revolutionary parts in disequilibrium and thereby blocked from a dramatic forward trajectory. Marxism seeks to massify the particles (the working class) and force the opposing bloc (the capitalist class) off the field, thus

Figure C—The Pre-Revolutionary Marxian Vision

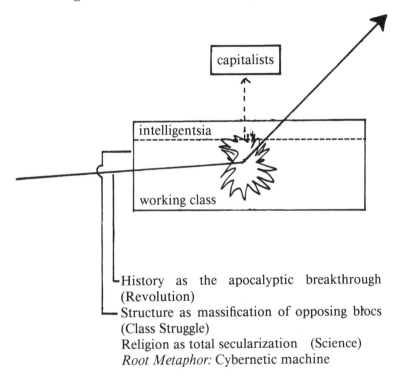

History as the apocalyptic breakthrough (Revolution)

Structure as massification of opposing blocs (Class Struggle)

Religion as total secularization   (Science)

Root Metaphor: Cybernetic machine

unleashing the revolutionary movement. In the post-revolution-ary phase, Marxism shifts to a system held in stasis by force from above. Similarly late liberalism begins to move toward this same model, shifting from a diffused equilibrium to one integrated by force from above (the move toward authoritarian liberalism). But the Newtonian paradigm in all of these versions misses funda-mental dimensions of the social reality, which the post-modern paradigm tries to recover.

THE SEARCH FOR A POST-MODERN VISION

In this final crisis of the modern drive and in the growing convergence of the two main modern ideologies, the search opens for a post-modern vision. Initially the search for this post-mod-ern vision takes the shape of a turn from one modern ideology to the other, depending on which ideology is dominant in one's environment.

Thus in the communist world critics often turn to liberalism as a source of freedom. They may do this in various degrees, some hoping to shift the whole system to capitalism, but more often only looking for a liberal or democratic revision of socialism.

Similarly in the capitalist world, critics often turn to Marx-ism as a vision of justice. Again this may occur in various degrees, sometimes simply accepting an orthodox Marxist view-point, but more often only as an attempt to create a more social-ist form of democracy.

Each ideology offers thus a creative partial critique of the other, even while they converge. But it is important to remember that each critique is only partial. Each still fails to critique itself, and above all fails to critique the common destructive tendencies of the mechanistic root metaphor underlying both ideologies in their late modern convergence. Each partial critique therefore only becomes truly creative if it opens to the wider search for a post-modern vision.

At this point, I would like to sketch the post-modern para-digm I perceive actually emerging in the praxis of the Catholic shift to the left. Theoretical articulation on this fresh praxis, distinguishing it as a post-liberal, post-Marxist, and post-modern form, seems yet to be accomplished. But that is the direction, I believe, toward which the praxis points. Again there is not space here to argue that this is indeed the direction, so my proposal remains still at the level of hypothesis. Nonetheless, let me now project what I view to be basic elements in this implicit post-modern paradigm.

(1) *History:* The classical view saw history as the repetitive biological cycle of birth and decay, yet containing within its soul a transcendent core of eternal truth protected by the rock-like institutions of civilization. The two modern ideologies broke with the classical heritage by turning the repetitive cycle into a linear arrow of progress (evolutionary or revolutionary) and dissolving the transcendent religious core of the civilization into secularization. Thus for the classical view the future was a continuation of the past and the conservation of eternal truth. For the modern view the future became a liberation from the past, and the discovery of new scientific truths. How then would a post-modern perspective differ?

I would propose that the post-modern vision is moving toward a truly dialectical view of history as on-going creation. Linking subversive memory with creative imagination, the new future emerges to challenge the present, but it remains a future rooted in the past. Reaching for the future entails tapping the past roots. Past and future thus form an ecology of the whole. Dynamic movement continues, not as rejection of the past, but as a deepening of its creative energy.

Such a truly dialectical view could be viewed in the figure of a spiral and is the prophetic biblical view of history. It taps the tradition to break the idolatry of the present and thereby deepen new creation in the future. It is not a closed circle, nor an uprooting arrow, but a holistic spiral.

(2) *Structure:* If roots and imagination are the focal points of the historical axis for the post-modern vision, community becomes the focal point of its structural axis. The social body is not a hierarchical body as in the classical ideology (where the lower existed for the higher). Nor is it simply a collection of New-

tonian particles (dispersed in a competitive equilibrium or massified as a single force) as in the modern ideologies. Rather, the parts exist in communion with each other, that is with discreet dignity for each, yet cooperating creatively as a whole. And above all, the communion is a creative communion, so that the whole becomes more than the sum of its parts, both structurally and historically.

The building of community is the foundation of the creative act. Community in turn unleashes its creativity by tapping its historical roots and freeing its prophetic imagination. Thus the historical and the structural principles are linked in a common and creative ecology.

Further the communion is not simply social (among humans) or religious (with the divine), but also natural (with the ecological matrix). Again the structural axis is founded on the same holistic or ecological principle as the historical one.

(3) *Religion:* For the classical ideology, the whole was sacral, but a sacrality flowing from the domination of the lower by the higher, and in the flight from history and rooted community. The modern ideologies destroyed this sacrality and substituted differentiation and secularization (an evolutionary destruction in liberalism, a revolutionary one in Marxism). For the post-modern paradigm, however, the sacred is restored but counterposed to domination and disclosed in the creative communion of spiritual matter across time and space. The sacred is revealed in the creative formation of natural, social, and religious communion, tapping the root and simultaneously opening the imagination.

The formation of community, tapping the root, exercising the creative imagination—these are the ultimately religious acts which begin to pervade and transform the whole human experience. The god of classical domination fades, as does the modern god of subjective privatization and autonomous secularization. What discloses power is the living Mystery revealing itself in ongoing creation and re-creation.

(4) *Root Metaphor:* The root metaphor of the classical premodern period was organic (the body), housing a fortified transcendent soul. The root metaphor of the modern period became mechanistic, initially only a physical machine in liberalism, later

a cybernetic machine in Marxism. The root metaphor of the post-modern period becomes the artistic creation expressed in the ecological communion of time and space.

There are many ways of describing this post-modern social and religious vision. Gibson Winter has referred to it as the rise of the artistic root metaphor, or the emergence of a creative society.[13] Others have highlighted the principle of community, and referred to a communitarian or even communitarian-socialist society.[14] Others have pointed to the end of secularism and referred to it as a specifically religious or theistic society.[15] Others have stressed the recovery of roots, and thus might describe it as a rooted society reacting against the uprooted and manipulative cosmopolitanism of late modernity.[16] Using the centrality of the ecological principle and embracing natural creation as well, some might describe it also as an ecological society.[17] In any case, and in every one, the pattern is post-modern.

One might ask where are these post-modern patterns to be found in the current praxis of the Catholic Church's shift to the left. Again there is not space to chronicle or argue them in this unfolding of the hypothesis, but I will make a few suggestions.

A general post-modern praxis might be argued from the two great Catholic challenges to modern ideologies—one against the capitalist form in the third world and the other against the communist form in Eastern Europe. (Note that both are peripheries of their respective superpowers, in effect modern Galilees). These two fundamental challenges have not been coordinated, and may even seem in some way opposed to each other. But I propose that they will increasingly converge in solidarity.

The new consciousness on the historical axis seems clear in the simultaneous unleashing of subversive memory and prophetic imagination. Latin American liberation theology recalls the journey of the poor, and imagines an alternative future. Polish Catholicism clings stubbornly to its traditional roots, and thereby projects a transformed future of Eastern Europe. The subversive past becomes a prophetic challenge to the present which unleashes the creative future. The new historical consciousness is more profound than simply "progressive."

On the structural axis, the core theme of community is abun-

Figure D—The Post-Modern Vision

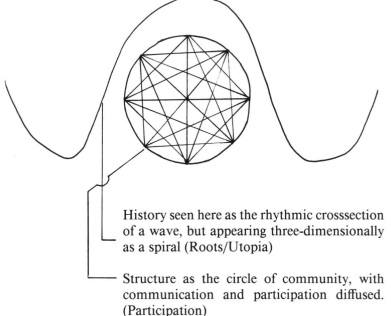

History seen here as the rhythmic crosssection of a wave, but appearing three-dimensionally as a spiral (Roots/Utopia)

Structure as the circle of community, with communication and participation diffused. (Participation)
Religion as the sacrality of creation and re-creation (Mystery)
Root Metaphor: The work of art

dantly clear in the pastoral priority of the basic Christian community (increasingly all over the world). Classical hierarchical models collapse, liberal individualism produces only loneliness, and Marxist massification proves destructive. The actual praxis of the shift to the left is not authoritarian, nor individualistic, nor massified, but precisely communitarian. And the focal energies of the Christian counter-culture are no longer on the state, but on the community. They may support a left leaning state, I propose, only to the degree that it builds on the community principle. The moment that breaks down, as happened long ago in Poland, I predict that the Christian counter-culture will begin to oppose even a left state.

On the religious axis, the core themes of creation and new creation can be seen in the rise of creation-oriented spiritualities, displacing the classical anti-creation spiritualities of spatial transcendence and repressive asceticism, and the modern anti-creation spiritualities of privatized pietism or holiness by technique. Of course the heritage of past spiritualities remains, but they need to be transformed and integrated into the primacy of the new creation orientation. One thinks of the writings of Matthew Fox and Thomas Berry.[18] Liberation theology is linked to this by the centrality of the exodus theme, not simply as negative emancipation, but as the biblical vision of new creation.

Chart I—Summary of Ideological Visions

VISION	HISTORY	STRUCTURE	RELIGION
Classical:	Circle	Hierarchy	Eternal Truth
Liberal:	Arrow (Evolution)	Competition	Privatization
Marxian:	Arrow (Revolution)	Massification	Secularization
Post-Modern:	Spiral	Community	Creation

In sum, I propose that the new praxis of the Catholic Church in its shift to the left contains implicitly a vision of history as the creative power of living tradition, of structure as the creativity of community across nature and humanity, and of religion as human participation in the on-going divine creation and re-creation.

ECUMENICAL IMPLICATIONS

This implicit rise of a post-modern praxis within the Catholic Church's shift to the left (and not only the Catholic Church by the way) suggests not simply a post-modern social and religious vision, but also a post-modern theological foundation for an ecumenical Christianity—dialectically sublating classical Catholic and modern Protestant insights.

The pre-modern classical vision and the initial liberal modern vision are sequentially linked with the theological foundations of classical Catholicism and modern Protestantism. The contemporary liberalization of Catholicism also draws on the liberal vision. But the roots and future of Christianity are not bound to these ideological incarnations. Indeed I would propose that a precisely new form of Catholicism, opening on an ecumenical synthesis, is being born out of this shift to the left.

On the historical axis, the new form of Catholicism retrieves a biblical vision of prophetic time—on one side subversive memory and on the other side the prophetic imagination. Both Passover and Eucharist recall the past in order to move toward the future. The prophets thus remember the creative energies of the past precisely to subvert the destructive present and to unleash the future as new creation. This is distinguished from the ahistorical contemplative gaze at the heart of classical Catholicism, and from the negative transcendence of God projected in modern Protestantism as the totally other Lordship of Jesus Christ standing in judgment over nature and history.

On the spatial axis, the vision retrieves the biblical model of a covenanted community. This is different than the hierarchical structure of religious domination which presided over classical

Catholicism, and from the fragmented cluster of individual conversions (like so many private contracts) which provided the structural model for modern Protestantism. Rather the community is called forth as a whole, and a non-hierarchical whole, that is, as a people. This is the model of the qahal, the synagogue, the ecclesia, the Church. Catholic clericalization and Protestant privatization are both perversions of this image. They destroy the community's creative power.

At the deepest level, this vision is a retrieval of the foundational doctrine of continuing creation and re-creation. This doctrine was suppressed by the hierarchical and cosmic vision of eternal truth in classical Catholicism. It was also suppressed by the modern Protestant fixation on negative condemnation and judgment.

The classical Catholic view tended to lose any dynamic sense of history, depoliticizing evil into private sin or an external civilization (e.g., Islam), and fixating the positive creative side in a static eternal now mediated by Christendom. The modern Protestant view by contrast destroyed the stasis, but only negatively—by elevating the judgmental side at the cost of the creative power of both nature and grace.

The post-modern Christian vision would represent thus a post-classical Catholic and post-modern Protestant theological position, that is, a truly new and profoundly ecumenical creation. Sin becomes the idolatry of the present revealed by negative judgment, but overthrown by tapping the positive tradition anew and unleashing the on-going and complementary creative power of nature and grace. The sense of dynamism and negative judgment is a Protestant legacy. The positive sense of the goodness of the tradition of history and the substances of nature, and their complementarity with grace, is a Catholic legacy. Synthesized they could represent a new historical stage of Christianity.

Thus the Church's opening to the left is not only post-Marxist and post-modern, but also ecumenical—a retrieval of the foundational biblical prophetic vision of on-going creation and new creation, repressed into stasis in the classical covenant of Catholicism with Greco-Roman culture, and negatively disfigured in the Protestant covenant with modernity.

Again this post-modern vision might be seen as tapping the recessive side of Marx's own thought, and certainly the recessive non-scientific side of the whole modern socialist tradition. I think especially of communitarian, religious, and even utopian orientations in socialist history. Indeed Gregory Baum's book *Catholics and Canadian Socialism,*[19] makes such a suggestion plausible. But this is the subject for another essay. My hope here has been simply to outline the hypothesis that the contemporary praxis of the Church's shift to the left contains implicitly a post-Marxist and post-modern social and religious vision, and a new ecumenical opening.

NOTES

1. See Paul Ricoeur, *Interpretation Theory: Discourse and the Surplus of Meaning,* Fort Worth, Texas, Texas University Press, 1976, especially Chapter IV; also Gibson Winter, *Liberating Creation: Foundations of Religious Social Ethics,* New York, Crossroad, 1981, pp. 80–84.

2. See for example, James Hitchcock, *Catholicism and Modernity: Confrontation or Capitulation,* New York, Crossroad, 1979. In a similar vein is Ralph Martin, *A Crisis of Truth: The Attack on Faith, Morality, and Mission in the Catholic Church,* Servant Books, Ann Arbor, Michigan, 1982.

3. Liberation theology is often seen as the leading edge of this encounter with an alleged surrender to Marxism. For an excellent review of the whole question, and an argument that liberation theology in fact is not Marxist but more biblical, see Arthur McGovern, *Marxism: An American Christian Perspective,* Maryknoll, NY, Orbis, 1980.

4. The most comprehensive American study of the Enlightenment is probably Peter Gay's two volumes, *The Enlightenment: An Interpretation,* both published by Norton, New York—Volume I, *The Rise of Modern Paganism,* 1966, and Volume II, *The Science of Freedom,* 1969.

5. This perspective constantly appears in the writings and speeches of Pope John Paul II. See for example his speech, "The Crisis of the West," given to a conference of German and Italian scholars on November 12.

6. See note 1.

7. The more noble side of this vision provides the foundation for a truly conservative critique of modernity. Its best expression can per-

haps be found in the writings of the late Christopher Dawson. See for example his essays edited by his thoughtful colleague John J. Mulloy, *Dynamics of World History,* LaSalle, Illinois, Sherwood Sugden, 1978. The essence of the conservative critique of modernity is the loss of transcendence by secularization.

8. An examination of the liberal vision can be found in Roberto Mangabeira Unger, *Knowledge of Politics,* New York, Free Press, 1975.

9. Perhaps the most comprehensive investigation of Marxism is Leszek Kolakowski, *Main Currents of Marxism,* Oxford University Press, New York, 1981 (3 volumes).

10. For one perspective on the internal tensions within Marxism, see Alvin Gouldner, *The Two Marxisms: Contradictions and Anomalies in the Development of Theory,* New York, Seabury, 1980.

11. See note 8, p. 10.

12. See Chapter IV of Peter Henriot, S.J. and Joe Holland, *Social Analysis: Linking Faith and Justice,* Maryknoll, Orbis Press, and Washington, DC, Center of Concern, 1983.

13. See note 1.

14. See Harry Boyte, *The Backyard Revolution,* Philadelphia, Temple University Press, 1981.

15. Houston Smith, *Beyond the Post-Modern Mind,* New York, Crossroad, 1982.

16. Simone Weil, *The Need for Roots,* Boston, Beacon Press, 1952.

17. See the various writings of Thomas Berry (available in mimeographed form from the Riverdale Research Center, Riverdale, New York).

18. See note 17; also Matthew Fox, *A Spirituality Named Compassion,* Minneapolis, Wiston Press, 1979.

19. Paulist Press, New York, 1980.

Rosemary Ruether

Theologizing from the Side of the "Other": Women, Blacks, Indians and Jews

Why is there a need to theologize from the side of the "other"? Is this simply adding new "frills" and supplements to the solid core of theology, as that has been established by many generations of accumulated theological tradition? In this essay I wish to argue that theologizing from the perspective of the "other" is a fundamental shift of perspective that throws the traditional systems of Christian theology into question. It looks at these systems from the perspective of the marginalized and oppressed people of history who have not been allowed to reflect theologically on their experience, whose experience has not been incorporated into traditional theology. These peoples have not only been exploited socially and economically, but they have been denigrated and/or rendered invisible in the dominant culture.

To the extent that theology has shared this cultural bias against marginated people, it has reinforced this denigration and justified this oppression. The dominant class (race, religion and gender) has done the theologizing and, in so doing, has explicitly or implicitly incorporated this social bias into its theology. Theologizing from the perspective of the other exposes this bias and renders it visible. Latin American liberation theology exposes the classical systems as Euro-centric, done from the perspective of the ruling classes of Europe and now of capitalist, industrialized countries.[1] Feminist theology exposes classical theology as sexist, done from the perspective of male dominance.[2] Black theology exposes classical theology as white theology, done from the perspective of Northern Europeans and Anglo-Saxons.[3] Jewish religious thinkers expose the anti-semitic bias in Christian theology. Native American religious thinkers expose not only the racial and Christian biases of the dominant theology, but also its denigration of "nature."[4]

Theologizing from the side of the "other" starts with a revolt of the "other" against objectification by the dominant, culture-defining class (race, gender, religion). Members of the marginated group declare themselves to be subjects, definers of their own identity and nature. They affirm themselves as authentically human, as children of God and heirs of promise. This does not mean that they regard themselves as sinless or infallible (although one of the dangers of theologizing from the side of the other may be reverse projection, a subject that we will take up later in this essay). Rather it simply means that they affirm themselves as persons, as centers of consciousness, and, from the vantage point of their own experience, name themselves and the world.

Since oppressed peoples have been the object of false naming, a large part of their experience has to do with this situation of objectification and oppression by the dominant group. They name themselves as authentically human, as subjects of history and culture, *against* those who have denied them this identity and role and who have named them as the "other." They criticize the ideological biases of the dominant theology that have been used to marginate and negate them, and, in so doing, they begin to glimpse an alternative theology. This alternative theology is not only one that is *expanded* to include them, but also is *transformed.* The hierarchical and dualistic systems of thought must be dismantled and reconstructed, so that these dualisms are no longer used to negate others.

Feminist theologians, black theologians, American Indian and Jewish religious thinkers (I change these terms here because the term "theology" itself is a Hellenistic-Christian construct and so does not precisely apply to non-Christians) are not only affirming their own authentic humanity, and naming themselves and their culture/religion as authentic means of revelation and redemption. They are redefining the names for sin. The false naming of the "other" that renders them invisible or as objects of oppression involves a false naming of sin. Marginated people are declared to be responsible for their own margination. They are said to have "sinned" and so their margination and oppression is justified as an appropriate expression of divine reprobation against them. The dominant group appropriates to itself not only authentic humanity (the *image* of God), but also the means of grace and redemption. The others are declared to be under divine judgment, and for this reason justly punished by their marginated position in the Church and in the social order.

The theologies of liberation throw off this false naming of sin which justifies injustice. They rename this projection of judgment upon the others as itself the real and most basic root of sin. The definitions of sin that justify oppression are demythologized and exposed as themselves sanctions of evil. Sin is thereby also recognized to be collective and historical, not merely private and individual. It is not primarily as individuals, but as members of groups, that theologians of the dominant culture have justified social bias against the others.

This does not mean that there is no personal responsibility for sin, but, rather, that this personal responsibility is embedded in a collective, historical situation. This means that much of this bias was carried on on the unconscious level. Insofar as theologians of the dominant group expressed this bias in an explicit and conscious way, they did so because they believed that this was "right," i.e., they were possessed by false consciousness. Thus the traditional Catholic definition of a sinful act as one that takes place when there is explicit recognition that the act is wrong and full consent of this will is not fully applicable here. In fact, this definition of sin is itself revealed to be biased by individualism.

We must situate the sin of oppressive false consciousness in the context of a larger understanding of sin, i.e., as Powers and Principalities, as systems of evil that we buy into so completely that they appear to be natural, right and divinely ordained. We name God and God's will, as well as authentic humanity, sin and redemption, from within the system of evil. Consequently, the reprobation of sin itself becomes a means of justifying sin and

God becomes a sanction of evil, i.e., the Creator of the Powers and Principalities.

In this essay I wish to illustrate the use of theological categories as sanctions of evil from the perspectives of four groups marginated by white Christendom: women, blacks, American Indians and Jews. Since the author herself belongs to only one of these groups, namely, women, she can only claim to make this criticism from "within" the condition of otherness in the case of women. The criticism of the biases of Christian theology against blacks, native Americans and Jews comes from dialogue with the experience of persons, especially critical religious thinkers, from within these groups.

Those who stand in the position of an "other" over against the dominant system of culture and theology can claim to have an element of "hermeneutical privilege" (to use a term from Latin American liberation theology[5]). The experience of otherness, as a woman, or as a Jew, or as a black or as a native American allows one to see the biases which remain invisible to the dominant group, or which appear to them to be natural, inevitable and divinely ordained. Once having learned to look at theology from the perspective of one of the marginated groups, one begins to recognize the general patterns of objectification and justification of oppression. But one cannot assume that being able to recognize the oppressive structures toward one group automatically sensitizes a person to all other oppressions. A critical feminist may be quite oblivious to class, racial or anti-semitic biases in her thought. Although the patterns of projection and oppression are similar (all coming from the same dominant group), each of these groups has its own historical particularity. They are not interchangeable. Their experiences of oppression are different. They each have alternative cultures and identities which are quite distinct from each other.

Thus oppressed groups must hear each other's stories. Each story is unique and different, despite common patterns that originate in their subjugation by the same dominant group. Only from the perspective of these many different kinds of otherness in dialogue with each other does one sense the full dimensions of the system of oppression and begin to name a more inclusive alternative. This is an ongoing process. There are many groups whose perspectives will not be included here, i.e., homosexuals, Asians. Thus no theology of otherness can claim to be itself the universal, inclusive system. Rather a process is started, but is still incomplete, of enlarging the compass of human solidarity.

GENDER OTHERNESS: FEMINIST THEOLOGY

It is not too extreme to say that women have been the most continually denigrated group within the Judaeo-Christian tradition. Their margination and oppression reaches back to the roots of biblical religion itself, and before. Although racist elements are also present in Scripture, the denigration of Africans and Indians, as specific groups, appears in Christian history and ideology only with modern Euro-American colonialism. Anti-semitism arises through the conflict of the religion of the "New Testament" with that which they define, in relationship to themselves, as the "Old Testament." For the oppression of women we have, so to speak, a more united "tradition," that flows through both Testaments and down through the centuries of Christian theology.

Two basic theological assertions underlie the denigration of women. First, women are declared secondary in the "order of creation," and thus "naturally servile" or in a state of subjection to the male who is their natural and divinely ordained "head." Second, women are declared to be "moral subversives." They possess not only a secondary, but a morally inferior human nature. They are more "weak willed," sensual and irrational than the male. This moral inferiority causes them to be more prone to sin, or, more specifically, to be the cause of "tempting" the male to sin. To use Augustine's phrase, they "drag the manly mind down from its heavenly heights to wallow in the flesh."[6] Therefore, they are not only under subjection according to the original order of creation, but this subjugation must be reinforced as "punishment" within the fallen order of sin. Women must be suppressed and kept in check, their physical and social mobility restricted. They must be veiled, secluded and kept in silence so that they will not subvert and corrupt the intellect and morals of the superior and normative member of the human species, the male.

The *locus classicus* in Scripture for this interpretation of woman as secondary in creation and morally subversive comes from the interpretation of Genesis 2–3 in post-Pauline theology in the New Testament, i.e., 1 Timothy 2:13–15. This post-Pauline interpretation of Genesis 2–3 is used by the author of 1 Timothy to exclude women from teaching authority in the Church, to name them as moral dangers through their "attractive" appearance and to define them as in a state of subjugation to the male both in society and in the Church. It may be noted here that neither the Hebrew Scriptures nor the Gospels make any use of this Genesis text as a myth of the aetiology of evil which holds women especially responsible for sin.

It is likely that the misogynist use of Genesis 2–3 begins in rabbinic thought during the inter-testamental period and is from thence picked up and incorporated into the Pauline concept of the fallen Adam by a post-Pauline Church which wishes to suppress the earlier participation of women in ministry that has been current in some of the early churches.[7] This does not mean that biblical Judaism did not believe that women's subjugation was divinely ordained. But they do not use Genesis 2–3 as a text for this purpose, and thus do not link women's social subjugation as directly with the aetiology of evil as does Christian theology.

This misogynist bias can be traced in the theological anthropology of classical Christianity in all its major branches. Thus, for example, Augustine believes that woman was naturally subject to man in the original order of creation. By symbolically·linking the male with mind and reason and woman with body and sensuality, Augustine even suggests that woman does not possess the image of God (authentic humanity) in herself, but only "when taken together with the male who is her head," although the male possesses the image of God in himself, apart from a relationship with woman.[8] Since Augustine believes that the original order of creation was one in which reason was totally in control of bodily sensuality, it follows that woman is both ontologically in a state of subjection and would have been so "naturally" in Paradise.

Sin consists of the revolt of the sensual against the rational self. Since woman represents the sensual self, she must be doubly kept (and keep herself) in subjection. The male remains, for Augustine, the chief actor in the drama of sin. He will not even allow that Eve could have "tempted" Adam, if he did not acquiesce. Woman must be controlled or shunned as the passive "occasion" of sin.[9]

In Aquinas, this theological anthropology has been worsened by the adoption of Aristotelian biology which allows Aquinas to argue that women are ontologically "defective." They are incomplete or imperfect in body, will and reason. As the weaker partner physically, morally and mentally, woman would have been naturally under subjection in the original order of creation. She is a necessary evil or imperfection in nature.[10] Under sin, she becomes additionally the occasion of temptation or morally subversion of the male, and so must be kept strictly suppressed, personally and socially. Preferably, she should be neither seen nor heard. She should be silent and invisible, carrying out her menial tasks behind the scenes, but not allowed to participate in the public male social or ecclesiastical orders.

This same theological anthropology is repeated with some variations by Luther and Calvin and carried down in the mainstream theologies of the Reformation. Luther argues (from the monastic tradition) that woman (Eve) was originally man's equal in Paradise, although the Lutheran tradition does not seem to have followed him in this assertion. But Luther uses this affirmation of original equality only to argue that Eve has fallen from this high estate through her role in the fall and is now in a state of subjugation as punishment for sin. Any restiveness or complaints against her subjugation become, for Luther, a sinful revolt against divine justice.[11]

Calvin and Calvinism, by contrast, argues for woman's subjugation in the original order of creation. But it does not follow Aquinas in suggesting that women are morally or spiritually inferior. Rather women are equal in "soul" to men. Their subjugation is a matter of divinely-appointed social "office" in the order of creation. When woman accepts her "place," she can be the "good wife" who is a beneficial helpmate to the male.[12] But when she revolts against her divinely-appointed place and wishes to teach in the Church, live her life independently or have authority over men, she subverts the social order and brings chaos and sin into the world.

Puritan theology of family life thus creates its "dark side." While it extols the "good wife" who meekly and piously accepts her husband's direction, even if he be harsh and cruel, it darkly suspects women of rebellious tendencies. These rebellious tendencies it regards as nothing less than the doorway by which the demonic enters the world. William Perkins, who extols the "good wife" in his treatise on the family, *Christian Deconomie* (1590), also wrote, in 1592, a *Discourse on the Dammed Art of Witchcraft*. In this he continues the medieval tradition that believes that women are more prone to the demonic and hence to witchcraft than men. He states that woman's proneness to witchcraft is due not only to her weak intellect and less firm control on her emotions, but also because she is prone to rebelliousness against her state of subjugation.

For Puritanism, the woman who departs from her divinely appointed place by rejecting male authority is not only a moral subversive, but a heretic and witch. She is a heretic because she is denying her divinely intended subjugation as clearly revealed in the Bible and taught by the Church. She is an incipient witch because she cooperates thereby with the devil in subverting the moral order of society. During the witchcraft trials in Massachusetts that raged from the 1660's to the end of the century, women were particularly examined for evidence of rebellion against male authority, in relation to either husbands, civil magistrates or ministers. Any proof that a woman was not strictly compliant in all these relationships was tantamount to proof of witchcraft.[13]

Thus Christian mythology about women not only justifies their social suppression, their reduction to servile labor in the home, denying them education, civil rights and participation in public leadership, either in society or the Church. It also projects on them its fears of "carnality" and of social subversion which it sees as the means for unleashing demonic powers. Woman is both the lesser and also the dangerous sex.

RELIGIOUS OTHERNESS: THE JEWS

Christian anti-semitism cannot be seen as simply another form of racism. Indeed, to speak of the "otherness" of the Jews as racial is a nineteenth century invention. Rather, Christian anti-semitism (or, more correctly, anti-Judaism) is a special form of religious antagonism that originates in the Christian claim to inherit the promises to Israel in the fulfilled messianic advent of Jesus as the Christ (Messiah), and the Jewish rejection of this claim.[14] Jews become the shadow side of Christian theological self-affirmation. They are the people of the Old Covenant and Old Testament which has been both superseded historically and spiritually perfected by the New Covenant. They represent the Old Adam, sinful, fallen humanity, over against the New Adam, Christ, in whose nature Christians share through faith and baptism.

Even worse, Jews are the Christ-killers, the representatives of the apostate self which rejected and killed the prophets and have rejected and killed God's final revelation in Christ. In so doing they have denied their own salvation, the redemption for which they themselves hoped. Until they repent, they have lost all hope. Judaism, for Christianity, has a pre-Christian past, but no future. The Jew survives as a religious anachronism and a sign of human refusal of faith, who must find his completion only by surrendering his Jewish identity into Christianity. He is allowed to continue to exist by God, but only in a state of reprobation and under divine curse, until he sees the light and converts to Christianity.

Christianity appoints itself the historical agent of this divine reprobation against the Jews. The Jews must not have any honor or authority in Christian society. They must never hold any social office where they are above Christians. They cannot proselytize. Their religious edifices must be mean and humble compared with the soaring Christian spires. They are marginated into ghettos, denied the normal range of economic employment, allowed to live in Christian lands only under the sufferance of Christian princes who use them for the hated social tasks of tax collectors and money lenders. They must submit to regular Christian conversion sermonizing.[15]

From this enforcement of reprobation as social, political and economic repression, Christian culture moves on to paranoia against the Jew. Jewish perfidiousness is a disease of the soul which might be catching. Jews contaminate Christian society. They plot against it in dark and devious ways. They seize the presence of Christ among Christians in the form of the Eucharistic wafer and skulk off with it to do magic against Christian souls. They gather in "cabals" to conspire against the Christian social order. They are in league with the devil. The very Messiah for whom they look, in rejection of the true Messiah, Christ, is really the devil. Any success or power of Jews in Christian society is thus both an offense against the superiority of Christianity which has superseded the Jew, but also a dangerous power that might open the gates of the New Jerusalem to the floodtide of demonic hosts.

This social denigration, together with paranoia, nurtured against the Jew in Christian civilization in sermon, theology and canon law, found its expression in continual rampages of Christian mobs, often led by fanatical priests and monks, against the Jewish ghettos. The Jew was continually harassed, massacred and expelled from Christian society, despite the official teaching that the Jew must continue to exist in Christian society until the "end of time" when Elijah would return and the Jew would finally acknowledge his error and embrace Christianity. The Jew, incomplete and spiritually superseded by Christianity, thus also becomes a cause of Christian incompleteness. As long as the Jew exists, salvation is incomplete.

The Jew is both despised as the apostate, perfidious self, but looked on with fascination as a source of occult and demonic power. In a sense he comes to hold the key to final redemption in Christian salvation history. When the Jew finally repents and accepts Christianity, the return of Christ will be near. Christian anti-Judaism has a particularly pathological character since its hatred and need for vengeance against the Jew is rooted in unrequited love. Christianity thus has a need both to punish and also "protect," i.e., maintain in existence, the Jew as the foil for its own theological identity and the key to its own final consummation.

Christian anti-Judaism originates essentially in religious ide-

ology. The Jew is the antagonist of Christian theological self-affirmation. It differs from other kinds of denigration of non-Christian religions, because Judaism, unlike Islam or Buddhism, is the
"father" of Christianity, or rather Christianity is the unacknowl-
edged "son and heir" of Judaism. The need to repudiate the
autonomy of Judaism and to vilify Jewish existence is based on
a fundamental insecurity in Christian identity about its status as
the authentic son and heir of Judaism. Until Judaism itself
affirms Christianity as its true "heir," Christian fulfillment is
incomplete. The rage of Christianity against the Jew is that the
Christian wants something from the Jew without which it cannot
be fulfilled, but which the Jew must ever withhold in order to
remain a Jew. This impasse in the relation of Judaism and Christianity has continued to the present day, ever taking new forms.

The social denigration of the Jew, the denial of public office,
denial of participation in the magistracy, army, law and university, the economic marginalization and exploitation, are secondary to this ideological need. They flow from the need to punish
the Jew, to demonstrate God's reprobation of the Jew on the
stage of history where Christianity reigns as God's new elect and
favorite. This need to punish, but also to "protect" for the day of
final vindication, constantly is in danger of bursting its limits, of
spilling over into pure genocide against the Jew which would
remove the Jew altogether from the stage of history.

In this sense Hitler is a Christian heretic who tried to carry
reprobation to the point of annihilation and thus to lose the Jewish presence altogether as the source of final vindication. Logically, the Christian church should have opposed Hitler at this
point of genocide. But Hitler concealed his full intentions and
portrayed his "final solution" as renewal of legal reprobation and
then as expulsion, both forms of denigration long practiced and
acceptable to Christians. Moreover, Christians were no longer as
clear about the difference between reprobation and annihilation
and so were not inclined to make careful inquiry as to Jewish
fate.

The paradox of Christian anti-Judaism is that it maintains
itself even in the absence of Jews. Fundamentally, it is internal
to Christian identity itself and so is not actually dependent on
the physical and social presence of Jews.

RACIAL OTHERNESS: BLACKS AND NATIVE AMERICANS

Racial discrimination enters more illegitimately into Christian theology and in relatively recent times, in contrast to sexism and anti-Judaism which are directly rooted in Christian Scripture. Racism comes into Christian theology through the back door of religious discrimination against non-Christians, combined with racist theories drawn from ancient and modern nationalism. Among Anglo-Saxons particularly there was a close connection between religious and national identity. Seventeenth century Englishmen believed that they were God's chosen people, the New Israel elected by God to purify the Church and combat the Spanish Catholic infidel.

This concept of the Anglo-Saxon as God's elect was heightened by the Puritan settlers in America, who saw themselves as analogous to ancient Israel's journey to the promised land to plant the New Zion in the wilderness.[16] Although originally the Puritans hoped to convert the Indians, their racial exclusiveness and unwillingness to incorporate the Indian into their communities (closely associated with their church) made this difficult. When the Indians took to the warpath against the settlers, this view of the possibility of Indian conversion was mostly dropped. Instead, the Indian came to be seen as the image of the unredeemed heathen whose dark skin was evidence of lack of divine grace within. Like the ancient Canaanites, God had intended to push aside (exterminate) those idol-worshipers in order to make way for God's people. The dark savage and the untamed wilderness both symnbolized fallen "nature" in the grip of the devil which God's people had been commissioned to conquer and subdue.

Although missionizing efforts continued, the primary view of the Indian in the North American continent became that of part of the wilderness that is destined to "disappear" as the continent was "tamed" by the whites.[18] The lower "natural" world of heathen humanity and nature is not so much "converted" as it is annihilated by a redemptive grace that comes "from above" and without any basis in "nature." This reformation view of the relationship of nature to grace aided the Anglo-Saxon Protestant in seeing the settlement of North America primarily as an imposition of a "higher" truth and reality by exterminating what is "lower," rather than any dialogue or amalgamation of the two cultures.

More elaborate and vehement racial theories developed in North America in relation to the enslaved African, who, unlike the Indian, was brought to America as a labor force. The Indian, whose destiny was to "disappear," along with the vanishing wilderness, could be romanticized. The Negro must be constantly restrained as an enslaved group within the white settlements. Like the Indians, blacks were, at first, thought of as heathen, and their dark color was seen as evidence of their lack of redeeming grace. The symbolism of light and dark, as color images of grace and sin, God and the devil, witnessed to the divine election of the white and the devil-gripped character of the black from the "dark" continent. At first, many white slave owners resisted the possibility that blacks could be converted or baptized, since this suggested that they might share white divine election and, even more, would become equals with whites in the fellowship of the Church.

However, missionaries convinced settlers that baptism could be separated from emancipation. The Negro was naturally an inferior and "childlike" creature who would be "protected" and civilized through Christianization. Bondage was a divinely appointed instrument for this task, and thus was essentially benevolent, like the rule of fathers over children and husbands over wives. The black would be taught to "obey his master" through the Gospel, and so baptism would create a docile and obedient slave who would see his subjugation to his master as analogous to his service to the white Father in heaven.[19]

During the nineteenth century, pseudo-scientific race theories began to supplement these concepts brought by religion. Some anthropologists of the Enlightenment rejected the biblical concept of universal descent through Adam and argued for separate origins of different races. Later, Darwin's concept of evolution was adopted to race theory to create a "ladder" or hierarchy of races, in which the white Anglo-Saxon or Teuton was the apex, and the Negro was the bottom. Both of these ideas were thought of as blasphemous and heretical by conservative Christians, but they were adopted by "enlightened" Christians who thought of themselves as progressive and open to "scientific truth." Whether as "separate species" or simply a lower state of human evolution, the Negro was seen as less fully human and more "beast-like" than the white, a kind of intermediary between ape and human.[20]

After the Civil War and the emancipation of the slaves in the United States, the more benign slave-holders' image of the Negro as an eternal "child" under the kindly paternal authority gave way to the more hostile view of the Negro as a "beast." This negative projection of "lower" characteristics of humans upon animals became the model for the white image of the Negro. The Negro was seen as both "stupid" (lacking intellectual capacities) and violently sensual. As such they must be both segregated from white society and forcibly repressed, particularly Negro males, in order to keep them from contaminating white society and assaulting white women. As stupid and beast-like, they were fitted only for hard physical labor.

CONCLUDING REFLECTIONS

It is evident that these patterns of religion and theology denigrate the humanity of the others, and deny them equal redeemability, and thereby justify their subjugation by the dominant class (race, gender, religion). We can differentiate two strata in these ideologies. One strata is directed primarily toward turning the others into a servile labor force. The primary concern is to exploit their labor without sharing with them the benefits of wealth, education, culture. In this aspect, the others are regarded as "stupid" and somatic types. They are denied the possession of equal capacities for education, intellectual prowess and culture. They are said to be more naturally sensual. They are described through parts of the body; women become all womb and tits, laborers are "hands," servants are "step 'n fetchit." Just as the mind must rule the body in the platonic Christian hierarchy, so the "mind people" (white ruling-class males) must rule the body

people. Since they partake of body and have little capacity for
mind, these people are naturally servile.

A second level of ideology projects upon the others demonic
characteristics. The others are thought of as sensual in the sense
of a sinful eroticism hostile to divine grace. They are materialistic
in an anti-spiritual way. They are prone to evil, their souls are in
the grip of the devil or they conspire with the devil to bring spiritual death to the Christian soul. They are like dirt, disease, ver-
min, crawling insects of the grave. This projection of the demonic
upon the other bursts the bounds of the use of the other for
exploitative labor. Instead, the other becomes a spiritual danger
that must be annihilated. The Indian must disappear; the Jew
must be expelled or annihilated; the witch must be burned in pur-
ifying fire. The other becomes the absolutely alien, the other
which has no place in creation at all, no right to exist, who must
be eliminated as part of a divine crusade of God and his people
against the demonic hosts of Satan. The first level of ideology
rationalizes economic exploitation. The second leads to outbursts of massacre which often contradicts this economic exploitation. The "other" as dangerous disease/devil wipes out the
other as useful body/beast.

In criticizing these patterns of subjugation and negation, and
developing theologies of liberation, those who theologize from
the perspective of the oppressed need to avoid two pitfalls,
reverse projection and schemes of "complementarity." In
schemes of complementarity, the others are still thought to have
a different human nature from the dominant group, but this different nature is romanticized and idealized, rather than denigrated. It might be noted here that in the dominant ideologies
about the "others," there is almost a certain "split image." The
others are both vilified, but also idealized. Women are both Eve
and the Virgin Mary, the good, pure and obedient "feminine."
Jews are both the scheming Shylock and the good Old Testament
patriarchs. Blacks are the kindly, wise Uncle Tom and Aunt Jem-
ima, as well as the black brute and whore. Indians are both the
savage devil and the noble savage, who preserves the qualities of
unfallen Eden. Schemes of complementarity make use of these
romanticizing patterns by which the others become repositories

of childlike, unfallen, innocence or good mothering and fathering traits.

In schemes of complementarity, women and men must complement each other as feminine and masculine. One is not lower than the other; indeed, if anything, the feminine is "higher," i.e., pure, altruistic, self-sacrificing. By assigning each their equal but "different" spheres, men and women can live in happy harmony. Similarly, the black is thought to possess innate "soul" powers and capacities for natural enjoyment, dance and rhythm which the over-rationalized white man has lost. Or the black is thought of as a Christ-like sufferer whose patient endurance and capacity for forgiveness will redeem the white man. Indians are thought to be in touch with the harmony of humanity and nature lost to the over-civilized. We must learn from them "nature wisdom." In Jewish-Christian relationship, complementarity takes the form of a revision of the two-covenant idea. The Jewish covenant has not been superseded. It is of permanent validity. But it is the particular covenant to one people, while to Christianity has been given the universal covenant to all people.

All these schemes truncate the humanity of the other while claiming to affirm the value of its "otherness." Jews lose the universal dimension of their identity and mission. Women, blacks and Indians are still denied rational intellect and the right to participate in the dominant social structures. They are ghettoized in rest and recreation spots for the redemption of the souls of alienated white males. The characteristics of otherness bestowed on women, blacks, Indians and Jews are those which the white man feels himself to lack. The others are segregated and confined to a "different" role in order to service this need for nurture and development of these suppressed characteristics of white males. But the agenda comes from the white male, not from the oppressed. The home, the ghetto and the reservation are romanticized as "return" to Eden and recovery of the repressed, but the oppressed still stay in these small reservations. They are still denied access to the means of power and participation in the dominant society.

The schemes of complementarity are seductive to oppressed people because there is some truth to the proposition that the white males have lost some human qualities which have been cultivated by oppressed people. But the agenda must be defined from the point of view of the affirmation of full humanity of the oppressed, not from the point of view of the white male who wishes to humanize himself by surrounding himself in his off-hours with complementary "nurturers" of his soul. The oppressed must press beyond complementarity to transformation. The walls that segregate the two groups must be torn down. In the process the cultural walls that assign one set of psychic characteristics to one group and another "opposite" set to another group must likewise be dismantled. We must claim our full humanity, as both particular and universal, both mind and body, both thinking and feeling, both acting and receiving, in a transformed relationship that allows these characteristics to be mutually and dynamically interconnected rather than related hierarchically. This demands both a new humanity and a new society. In claiming the full and unique humanity of each person and each people, one must also create a new social system that is not exploitative.

In this struggle to dismantle the oppressive social order and build a new, just society, the oppressed may be moved by anger and frustration toward reverse projection. The dominant group comes to be seen as innately evil and oppressive. A radical, separatist stage of the liberation struggle projects upon the ruling class (race, gender) the demonic face of all the accumulated evils and oppressions that they have suffered through the centuries. This face of accumulated injustice is not seen as a power system in which members of the dominant group are caught as well, socialized from infancy into their roles, without either understanding or fully consenting to the evil effects of the system upon others. Rather, this evil is attributed to the "nature" of the rulers as a gender, race or hereditary caste group. Males are seen as "naturally" aggressive, warlike, violent and sadistic toward those weaker than themselves. Whites are innately oppressive, exploitative, unfeeling. The white ruling-class male is held to be innately incapable of mutual and inclusive relations with women, with non-white races.

Once historical systems of evil are confused with the innate "nature" of rulers, then, in effect, the capacity for a good humanity is denied to them ontologically, as human beings. It becomes impossible for persons from the two groups to make coalitions with each other for a mutual common end of social justice. "After the revolution," the former rulers must be expelled or annihilated. One cannot create a new system in which men and women, blacks and whites can live in justice together. If a revolution of the oppressed should succeed, it will tend to follow a path of revenge and humiliation against the former rulers. This confusion of persons and systems is fueled by the fact that the members of former ruling classes often still have great power in larger international systems of privilege, i.e., the system of race, class and gender privilege is not totally overthrown.

The greatest danger in this tendency to reverse projection is not just the harm that may be done to former rulers. The really "big" culprits usually have options for comfortable escape. Rather, the primary casualty tends to be the liberation movement itself which becomes dehumanized and loses its inclusive vision through dehumanizing the "enemy." Social evil is projected entirely onto the enemy group, and so the liberation movement not only rejects their humanity, but also loses its own capacity for balanced self-criticism. It becomes rigid and doctrinaire. It becomes paranoid toward enemies within, often not without justification. The liberation party begins to become a caricature of that which they are fighting, rather than a humanizing alternative. It is very difficult to keep this reversal from taking place. The violent and subversive efforts of the rulers to maintain· their own power constantly feeds and justifies this negativity. Those who reject the vision of an inclusive humanity for reverse demonization of the enemy are seen as the "true radicals" who are willing to be ruthless and "effective."

It is precisely at this point that the convictions of authentic religious faith becomes most relevant for the liberation struggle. Only those who, in struggling against evil in others, keep constantly before their eyes their own capacity to sin can also continue to strive for a new world where the dividing wall of antagonism is broken down between groups. A more just system of social relations can be built only by those who are clear that the oppressors who must be dethroned are not only the former oppressors of the old ruling class, but also the new oppressors that they themselves may become.

NOTES

1. Enrique Dussel, *A History of the Church in Latin America: Colonialism to Liberation (1492–1979)*. Trans. and revised, Alan Neely. Eerdmans: Grand Rapids, MI, 1982.

2. Rosemary Ruether, *Sexism and God-Talk: Toward a Feminist Theology*. Boston: Beacon, 1983, pp. 13, 18–20.

3. James H. Cone, *A Black Theology of Liberation*. Philadelphia: J. B. Lippincott, 1970, pp. 89–90.

4. Vine Deloria, *God Is Red*. New York: Grosset and Dunlop, 1973, pp. 57–74.

5. See Robert McAfee Brown, *Gustavo Gutierrez: Makers of Contemporary Theology Series*. Atlanta: John Knox Press, 1980, pp. 57–58.

6. Augustine, *Soliloquies* 1, 10.

7. Elisabeth Schüssler Fiorenza, *In Memory of Her: A Feminist Reconstruction of Christian Origins*. New York: Crossroad, 1983.

8. Augustine, *De Trinitate* 7, 7, 10.

9. Rosemary Ruether, "Misogynism and Virginal Feminism in the Fathers of the Church." in R. Ruether, ed., *Religion and Sexism: Images of Women in the Jewish and Christian Traditions*. New York: Simon and Schuster, 1974, pp. 156–158.

10. Thomas Aquinas, *Summa Theologica,* pt. I, q. 92, art. 1. See also Kari Børresen, *op. cit.,* pp. 142–242.

11. Martin Luther, Lectures on Genesis, in *Luther's Works,* Vol. I, Jaroslav Pelikan, ed. St. Louis: Concordia Press, 1958, pp. 115, 202–203.

12. Edmund S. Morgan, *The Puritan Family: Religion and Domestic Relations in Seventeenth Century New England*. Westport, Conn.: Greenwood Press, 1980, pp. 17–21.

13. See Rosemary Skinner Keller, "New England Women: Ideology and Experience in First Generation Puritanism, 1630–1650," in R. Keller and R. Ruether, eds., *Women and Religion in America: The Colonial and Revolutionary Periods: A Documentary History*. San Francisco:

Harper and Row, 1983, ch. 4. See also Carol Karlsen, *The Devil in the Shape of a Woman.* Ph.D. Diss., Yale University, 1980.

14. Rosemary Ruether, *Faith and Fratricide: The Theological Roots of Anti-Semitism.* New York: Seabury Press, 1974, pp. 64–66 and *passim.*

15. *Ibid.,* pp. 184–214.

16. See Ernest Lee Tuveson, *Redeemer Nation: The Idea of America's Millennial Role.* Chicago University Press, 1968, pp. 137–186.

17. Thomas F. Grosset, *Race: The History of an Idea in America.* New York: Schocken, 1965, pp. 18–26. See also Richard Slotkin, *Regeneration Through Violence: The Mythology of the American Frontier, 1600–1860.* Middletown, Conn.: Wesleyan University Press, 1973, pp. 153–154 and *passim.*

18. *Ibid.,* Grosset, pp. 228–252. On page 243 Grosset cites a speech by Oliver Wendell Holmes in 1855 in which he says, of the inevitable extermination of the Indian through the forces of civilization: "And so the red-crayon sketch is rubbed out and the canvas is ready for a picture of mankind a little more like God's own image."

19. In the pro-slavery literature in the United States in the antebellum period it is commonly argued that slavery is both natural and divinely ordained and corresponds to the paternal government of fathers over children. See Frederick Augustus Ross, *Slavery Ordained of God* (1857), reprint: Miami: Mnemosyne Publishers, 1969.

20. *Op. cit.,* Grosset, pp. 54–83, 144–197.

Matthew L. Lamb

Political Theology and Metaphysics

The achievements of Gregory Baum are impressive, expressing his remarkable commitments to innovation and tradition. His life and work reflect an unusual sensitivity to the meanings and values inherent in both a cherished past and a present need for change. Jewish and Christian, Catholic and ecumenical, Freudian and Marxist, papal and socialist currents converge creatively in Baum's political theology. His works chart new possibilities for human and religious living within the context of recovering and criticizing central, and oft forgotten, features of these many currents. It is a privilege to contribute to this *Festschrift* honoring Gregory Baum. In the spirit of his commitments to innovation and tradition, I shall address some basic questions on a critical recovery of metaphysics within the theory and practice of political theology.

WHY METAPHYSICS TODAY?

At first glance it would appear that metaphysics plays practically no role in contemporary political or liberation theologies. After all, does not political theology acknowledge how the Enlightenment radically criticized traditional metaphysical reason? Johann B. Metz remarks on the hiddenness of the future in traditional metaphysics. More recently he indicates how the Enlightenment created a cognitive consensus on the basis of a positivist or empiricist practice of reason which, while denigrating metaphysics, reinforced a dominative use of empirical rationality over against nature for the sake of market economies.[1]

Indeed, Metz acknowledges how efforts to recover the memory of past metaphysical insights could subversively link metaphysics and history in a "liberating practical critique" of the one-dimensional domination of society by modern empiricist rationality with its market mechanisms.[2] This is reminiscent of Adorno's meditations on metaphysics at the end of *Negative Dialectics.*

Is this, however, only a concern of European political theology? There appears to be an absence of metaphysics in liberation theology. In general, liberation theology might be differentiated in terms of the forms of domination it seeks to overcome. Thus it is concerned with concretely transcending sexism (feminist), racism (black, native American), classism (Latin American, Latino-American), militarism (pacifist, nuclear pacifist), or technocentrism (environmentalist).[3] All these forms of liberation theology appear to engage in theological reflection without any explicit appeals to metaphysics. Metaphysics, and philosophy generally, seem replaced by critical and creative uses of contemporary social sciences and critical scholarship. Gustavo Gutierrez calls attention to how reason today has many other manifestations than those found in philosophy and metaphysics.[4] Juan L. Segundo mentions how liberation theology "cannot simply drag out metaphysical or universal questions" if it is going to respond to the pressing issues of global suffering and oppression.[5] Cornel West discounts the need for apodictic intellectual "grounds" or philosophical "foundations" in his fine articulation of an Afro-American liberation theology.[6] Rosemary Ruether and Letty Russell point out how feminist liberation theology is "inductive" and committed to multi-disciplinary approaches, rather than following the patterns of deductive reasoning from metaphysical first principles.[7] John Cobb calls attention to the importance of overcoming the substantialist metaphysics in any adequate ecological liberation perspective.[8]

Why, then, should we be concerned with metaphysics? Several reasons come to mind. First, political and liberation theologians are not anti-metaphysical. We have not followed the typically modern trend of writing long obituaries on "the end of metaphysics." Indeed, some of us find metaphysical categories helpful in articulating our concerns for social transformation. For example, Enrique Dussel takes up Emmanuel Levinas' notions of "totality" and "the other" in order to elucidate the geopolitical patterns of repressive imperial totalities and the challenge posed to them by the otherness of the peripheral, exploited countries.[9] Another example is John Cobb's transposition of process metaphysical categories in terms of the values involved in ecological and feminist liberation theologies.[10] A careful reading of political and liberation theologians would indicate how the type of deductivist metaphysics which increasingly deformed Christian theologies from the fourteenth century onward is rejected, but that metaphysical reflection is not identified with such a derailed metaphysics.

Second, these theologians are very critical of the modernist project in general. August Comte and Karl Marx, along with almost all representative writers in modernist Western culture, would claim an inherent contradiction between "liberation" and "theology." This was because they tended to identify theology with ideological legitimations of repressive, dominative power. Comte's famous law of the three stages envisaged humanity passing through a first stage of theology and a second one of metaphysics to the typically modern stage of positive philosophy and science. More dialectically, Marx criticized theology and metaphysics as idealist legitimations of basically oppressive socio-economic forces and relations of production. Political and liberation theologians are "post-modern" in the sense that religion and theology are not identified with the past and present uses of religion to legitimate ideologically such repressive social structures.[11] Instead, religion and theology can be critically recovered as prophetic denunciations of unjust and inhumane social structures. Hence, just as liberation theologies are critically recovering theology within a liberative context, so metaphysics can be recovered critically within such a liberative context.

A third and final reason for doing metaphysics today regards the intellectual dimensions of the liberation theological projects. These projects are rooted in the pastoral praxis of many thousands of Christian communities around the globe living in solidarity with the poor, with women, children and the elderly dependent upon women, with non-white races, with environmentalists, and with the defenseless and pacifists. These communities are appropriating, or making our own, the major texts and traditions of Christianity in order to help us transcend the sinful injustices of classism, sexism, racism, technocentrism, and militarism. Although these communal pastoral contexts and projects are minorities when compared to the larger populations which do not challenge past and present ways of living, these communities are creative minorities engaged in processes of transforming, or radically changing, the worlds in which they live. Such minorities have universal significance. The intellectual dimensions of these projects usually involve both a critical recovery of Christian texts and traditions, as well as the use of contemporary scientific and scholarly modes of reflection. Liberation theologians are challenged to understand both the particular and local contexts of their communities and, by the very dynamics of these communal efforts at transcending injustice, to relate those efforts to the whole of humankind. As Rosemary Ruether has written:

> Theologians today must be even more willing to dissolve the traditional perimeters of their "field," its sources and content, in order to rise to the task of sketching the horizon of human liberation in its fully redemptive context. If theology is really to speak meaningfully about the mediating point between the "is" and the "ought" of human life, then it takes as its base the entire human project, in the histories of the cultures of many peoples and in the diverse sciences of human activities, and finds in this total spectrum the framework for asking the ultimate questions about the *humanum;* its fall and its redemption.[12]

This multi-disciplinary generalization of the theological task could be enhanced and greatly aided by a metaphysics engaged in an open and ongoing project of understanding the entire human project by trying to penetrate, transform, and unify the diverse fields of human knowledge and action as a "framework for asking the ultimate questions about the *humanum*."

Admittedly, this notion of metaphysics is somewhat unusual, but certainly no more so than the notion of liberation theology was several decades ago. A liberation metaphysics would not have the immediate pastoral implications and contexts within which liberation theology emerged. Rather, it would be a "second order" type of reflection practiced by those engaged as "organic intellectuals" (Gramsci) in the cognitive or noetic dimensions of the liberation movements. In a mediated fashion, however, liberation metaphysics would have many theological and pastoral implications. Political and liberation theologians not uncommonly confront two different, if related, sets of criticisms. From some colleagues within theology come criticisms of a "political reductionism" insofar as these theologians are misunderstood as advocating a typically Enlightenment denial, or modernist neglect, of the traditional Christian affirmations of humanity's ontological "fallen" or "sinful" condition and God's transcendent and healing grace. Political and liberation theologians are criticized for relying too heavily on modern social sciences, thereby "materializing" Christian teachings and symbols in socio-temporal ways, as though struggling for more just and humane social orders were identified totally with the kingdom of God proclaimed by Christ.

From other colleagues within critical social science or liberation movements come criticisms of "theological idealism" insofar as political or liberation theologians are misunderstood as apologists for a Christianity which seems irremediably identified with dehumanizing and oppressive economic, social, and cultural structures. Liberation theologians are criticized for being too preoccupied with specifically theological problems, thereby "spiritualizing" categories such as "option for the poor" or "solidarity with the victims of history" in such a way that the concrete struggles for justice by the poor and the victims are hampered or neutralized. For one group of critics liberation theologians are too political, for another group they are too theological.[13]

TASKS OF A LIBERATION METAPHYSICS

This situation points to the need of articulating more explicitly the *logos* of liberation theology. The multi-disciplinary tasks mentioned by Ruether have to date involved the creative cross-fertilization of biblical and historical theological research with categories derived from social and psychological studies regarding sexism, racism, classism, militarism, and technocentrism. Just as liberation provides new perspectives on past and present practices of religious faith, so liberation provides new perspectives on past and present practices of reason. In articulating liberative perspectives and practices of reason, there are ultimate questions about the *humanum* which cannot simply be brushed aside. Catholic political and liberation theologians are especially challenged by their traditions on faith and reason to spell out the implications of their liberative understandings of faith in terms of a transformative understanding and appropriation of reason. This is already going forward in political and liberation theologies with their various efforts to understand and critically appropriate the methods and results of human and social sciences, as well as historical and literary criticism.

The movements among Christian and other religious believers for economic, political, social, and cultural transformations in solidarity with the poor and oppressed, along with the theoretical or theological works inspired by these movements, pose serious questions to modern secularist atheism. Karl Marx himself distinguished between a twofold set of methods in regard to emancipatory science or knowledge. The first set involves what Marx called *Forschungsmethode* in which inquiry and investigation would be "severely realistic" in their efforts to observe and critically investigate the manifold contexts of human and social phenomena. This is the phase of research and analysis. It is crucial, not only for indicating how Marx paid tribute to the empirical thrust of the early Enlightenment, but also for an understanding of how emancipatory science requires concrete contextualization. Such concrete and empirical methods of analysis, however, lead gradually to a second phase or set of methods.

Marx called them dialectical *Darstellungsmethode* in which the
results from the multiplicity of empirical analyses would be dialectically fashioned into conceptual syntheses in order to understand the dialectical relationships between many disparate concrete contexts uncovered in the analytic phase. Empirical
analyses of concrete contexts does not, therefore, leave us with
unrelated results in a kind of empiricist or positivist relativism.
Rather, for Marx, they are to be complemented by dialectical
syntheses in which there is a movement from broad conceptual
presentations or syntheses to contextual reconstructions in the
light of those synthetic concepts.[14] Marx's criticism of Hegel was,
in effect, that he failed to attend to the need of working up from
("Verarbeitung") concrete historical processes through empirical
analysis and research *prior* to the elaboration of dialectical synthesis. By wrongly beginning with generalized conceptual
syntheses, Hegel "mystified the dialectic," mistaking concrete
reality as nothing more than "a product of a self-generating concept or idea" which, as thought, was cut off from the first phase
of analysis. Thus Marx aimed at avoiding not only the relativism
of empiricism, but also the absolutism of idealism. The many
concrete contexts of scientific or cognitive analysis would gradually lead to ever more comprehensive dialectical syntheses,
which would in turn return to the concrete contexts in efforts at
dialectical reconstructions of those contexts in order to transform
them.[15]

The sketches Marx has provided in regard to his twofold set
of methods indicate how he attempted to link empirical and dialectical approaches in the service of transformative praxis. There
is a very obvious movement in Marx's distinct orientations: his
first phase is from the analyses of the multiplicity of concrete,
empirically diverse, situations toward a second phase of ever
more adequate conceptual reconstructions and dialectical
syntheses, which, once they are reached, return to the empirical
data in efforts to offer dialectical explanations capable of guiding
the praxis of changing or transforming those situations. The first
phase moves from experience of the concretely real toward dialectical consciousness and knowledge, which then returns to
experience informed by this consciousness and knowledge.

Marx's method, therefore, was not naively materialist. His criticisms of philosophy and metaphysics as idealist were not aimed against consciousness and knowledge as dialectically engaged in analyzing and synthesizing concrete situations. Rather those criticisms were aimed at the conceptualism which cut off consciousness and knowledge from such concrete engagements. Metaphysicians, Marx observed in *The Poverty of Philosophy,* conceptually strip concrete beings of all their particularities and think they are thereby getting nearer the essential core of such beings. This is "the language of pure reason" which impoverishes reality by dint of abstractions which transform everything into logical categories:

> Thus the metaphysicians who, in making these abstractions, think they are making analyses, and who, the more they detach themselves from things, imagine themselves to be getting all the nearer to the point of penetrating to their core—these metaphysicians in turn are right in saying that things here below are embroideries of which the logical categories constitute the canvas. This is what distinguishes the philosopher from the Christian. The Christian, in spite of logic, has only one incarnation of the *Logos;* with the philosopher there is no end to incarnations. If all that exists . . . can be reduced by abstraction to a logical category—if the whole real world can be drowned thus in a world of abstractions, in the world of logical categories—who need be astonished at it?[16]

Metaphysicians, for Marx, only "think they are making analyses" whereas in fact they are avoiding the empirical *Forschungsmethode* relative to the real world of nature and history, and, as a consequence, are caught up in impoverished conceptualistic methods incapable of truly presenting *(Darstellung)* the concrete intelligibilities constitutive of "the whole real world."

In relating Marx's comments in 1873 about his twofold set of methods to his earlier reflections on philosophy and religion, important insights emerge. First, in Marx's own praxis of analyzing the alienations of modern capitalist societies he is convinced that he is not caught in those alienations. His empirical methods of research have enabled him, as he states in 1873, to discover the concrete intelligibilities within social and historical processes which, in the conceptualism of Hegel, were wrapped in the mystified language of impoverishing abstractions. Yet these abstractions are not meaningless. They contain dialectical insights which can be demystified through empirical analyses and dialectical syntheses which discover the concrete and contradictory dynamics of the real world.

Second, this conjunction of the late and early Marx also indicates how Marx presupposed that "the whole real world" *is* intelligible in its manifold concrete and contradictory dynamics. Marx uses the language of discovery to differentiate his methods of analysis and dialectical synthesis from the positions of Hegel and the Hegelianism of right and left. Marx's discovery of the intelligible "laws governing the emergence, existence, development, and demise of given social organisms and their replacement by another form of social organization" took the intelligibility of Hegelian *Geist* and transposed its dialectics into the social history of humankind as "species-being." The conceptualism of German idealism is materialized in the concrete and contradictory dynamics of human societies laboring for their existence within the matrix of nature. The intelligibility of the real world is not, for Marx, an intelligible ordering of the cosmos and history which only requires the passive contemplation of a metaphysical spectator or theorist. Modern science, both natural and human, broke such a spell once and for all in the West.

For Marx the intelligibility of history was both to be discovered and to be realized by human subjects. Indeed, what has received too little attention in the libraries of Marxian studies is how the intelligibility of history was closely related to Marx's critique of religion and the expressivism of German Romanticism from Herder and Humboldt, through Schiller and Schelling, to Hegel and the Hegelians.

For Marx, as I mentioned, liberation theology would be a contradiction in terms. Religion for Marx, as Gregory Baum has indicated, is "always false consciousness, reflecting and protecting the injustices of the present social order. For Marx religion was the supreme legitimation of the structures of domination in human society."[17] Liberation could only occur as freedom *from* religion since religion is the "encyclopedic compendium" and "fantastic realization" of human being as alienated from its genuine species-being, as alienated from its true reality. Marx devoted little time or energy to a critique of religion. In his view this had already been accomplished. Philosophically, Hegel had sublated religion into the absolute knowledge of philosophy, which sublation was then criticized as human projective desire in Feuerbach's reassertion of reality as materialist. Politically, modern civil societies were already dismantling the sacralist pretensions of Christendom. Scientifically, the idealism of German philosophy, which was for Marx the last refuge of Christian theology, was giving way to the materialism and empiricism of natural sciences and social sciences. The "critique of heaven," in which modern sciences and societies were already engaged, had only to be complemented and radicalized by the "critique of earth" in terms of unmasking the alienations operative in modern capitalist societies and cultures.

Contemporary political and liberation theologies spring from major shifts away from the philosophical, political, and scientific contexts in which Marx lived and worked. Linguistically and socially it is often difficult for North American readers of Marx to appreciate how drastically the "option for the poor" among Christian churches reverses the understanding Marx had of Christianity. Indeed, Marx rarely, if ever, wrote of "Christianity" since German, to this day, tends to use the word "Christentum" rather than "Christenheit." Whereas "Christenheit" denotes the totality of Christians, "Christentum" connotes the historical and social mediations of Christian teachings and practices. It is somewhere between our "Christianity" and our "Christendom." While Anglo-American usage reflects the pluralism within Western Christianity since the Reformation, German usage tended to continue to accent the social and political mediations whereby even the Reformation led to two opposing sets of such mediations. On the one hand, Roman Catholicism continued to rely upon the vestiges of the "Holy Roman Empire" and European monarchies or aristocracies, while, on the other hand, Protestant churches tended to appeal to the emergent nation states and nationalisms.

Thus Johann Gottfried von Herder, in his influential *Ideen zur Philosophie der Geschichte der Menschheit,* written between 1784–91, depicts the heavy handed authoritarianism of Catholic or "Romish" hierarchies in the course of European history.

> In every movement the church was the fixed centre of the universe. The Roman political supremacy might employ whatever was conducive to this object: war and devastation, fire and sword, death and imprisonment, forged writings, perjury on the holy sacrament, inquisitorial tribunals and interdictions, poverty and disgrace, temporal and eternal misery.[18]

As Charles Taylor has indicated, Herder was decisive in shifting German culture away from the early Enlightenment tendency to interpret humanity and history in the extrinsicist categories of the natural sciences. Herder was one of the pioneers in the expressivism of German Romanticism which began interpreting humanity and history as the unfolding of desires and feelings within human beings as subjects or agents within history.[19] Hegel and the Hegelians of both right and left pursued this expressivism, even when they broke with Romanticism and initiated the second phase of the Enlightenment. They continually presupposed the expressivist framework in formulating the many ways in which humanity expresses itself in history, where the basic paradigm was human beings as knowing subjects.[20] History expressed the manifold progression of humankind's education into what Herder, and the Hegelians, termed the cultivation of reason.

Ludwig Feuerbach's *Das Wesen des Christentums* in 1843 marked a new stage in this expressivist interpretation of Christendom. The inner essence of Christendom was carefully culled from the manifold, and, to Herder, often barbaric, historical manifestations of Christian political domination and authoritarianism. Hegel's dialectical efforts to sublate Christendom into the movements of absolute knowledge from art through religion to philosophy as reason, were reversed under the aegis of empirically sensuous human knowing. Similar to August Comte's famous law of the three stages, by which history moved from religion through metaphysics to positivist knowing, Feuerbach interpreted Christendom, and religion generally, as the childhood of humankind. The essence of Christendom was not, however, a realization of the past but of the present, in its movement into the future. For the Divine attributes which humans formerly attributed to God were only the projections of the deepest human desires. The real is not a spiritual ideal but spiritual ideals are but estranged desires of sensible—and so real—human beings in space and time.

> The mystery of the inexhaustible fullness of divine attributes is therefore nothing other than the mystery of the human essence in its unending differences, in its unending and yet sensibly perceivable attributes. For only in empirical sensuousness (Sinnlichkeit), only in space and time, does an unending essence or being (Wesen), in its unending variety of attributes, occur.[21]

Feuerbach provided an expressivist framework in which a completely secularist unfolding of human knowledge could make its own the positive attributes of religion and Christianity. What one misses in Feuerbach, however, is the concern of a Herder for the deformations of Christendom. Feuerbach's more contemplative materialism could not account for the *contradictions* between the essence of Christendom and its many social and historical manifestations.

Marx caught this deficiency in Feuerbach. Marx maintained the expressivist framework, only he transformed it by shifting from the paradigm of the historical unfolding of human knowing subjects to a paradigm of the historical unfolding of human working subjects. Marx judged that Feuerbach had successfully resolved the world of religious self-estrangement into its properly secularist basis. Yet such secularism could not be content with Feuerbach's merely contemplative and optimistic materialism.

> For the fact that the secular basis lifts off from itself and establishes itself in the clouds as an independent realm can only be explained by the inner strife and intrinsic contradictoriness of

this secular basis. The latter must itself, therefore, first be understood in its contradiction and then, by the removal of the contradiction, revolutionized in practice.[22]

Marx's critique of religion began, therefore, with the cognitive presupposition common to the left-wing Hegelians. Reality is essentially spatio-temporal and can only be genuinely known as such. The reality of human desire is a purely secularist and sensuous phenomenon. Where Marx differed was in recognizing that this secularist foundation is intrinsically contradictory and torn by inner strife. The optimism of the expressivist framework is not completely repudiated. Instead it is transformed from an attitude of idealist contemplative sense intuition of secular, material progress to an attitude of materialist practical and sensuous engagement in transformative or revolutionary praxis. Although the secular basis is riddled with contradictions, Marx does not accept any "inevitability" of such contradictions. For once those contradictions "are understood" they can be removed by praxis.

The expressivist framework provided Marx with a normative orientation in terms of the intelligibility of history; it had, as Jürgen Habermas has mentioned, enabled Marx to differentiate

between an *objectification* of essential powers and their *alienation,* between a satisfied praxis that returns to itself, and a praxis that is impeded and fragmented.[23]

But from whence come the desires which are, at the very least, utopian beyond imagination? The expressivist framework in Marx makes only a truncated turn to the subject as the species-being of humankind.

It is precisely this truncated, or half-hearted, character of Marx's normative expressivism which political and liberation theologies challenge. For they are relentlessly committed to criticize both the *sacralism* of pre-modern Christian and religious traditions, in which these were used to legitimate dominative power relationships, as well as the *secularism* of modern industrialized societies, in which secularist ideologies are used to legitimate dominative power relationships. The expressivist frame-work, from the young Hegelians onward, simply presupposed that "Christentum" was irredeemably identified with dominative power relationships, that the sacred would only be invoked to legitimate the status quo of such relationships. Religion could only be a sacralism, a "sacred canopy" both concealing domina-tion and distracting victims from their real sufferings. The spiri-tual and theological renewal, articulated by political and libera-tion theologies, in which a sacred discontent with the myriad forms of social injustice finds its inspiration within dialectical recoveries of biblical and religious traditions, has uncovered the *contradictions* within the sacral and the secular basis of social living.

Indeed, insofar as reason is essentially practical, essentially reason yet to be realized in history and society by continually criticizing and transforming the irrationalities of injustice, to that extent political and liberation theologies are beginning to form new creative relationships between faith and reason. Elsewhere I have analyzed both the cognitive and the social dimensions of these newly forming relationships.[24] Political and liberation the-ologies are not merely conceptual activities, they are engaged in both the methods of analytic research and synthetic presentations relative to the increasing engagements of Christians and believ-ers, personally and institutionally, in the ongoing struggles for social justice. In the course of these intellectual efforts, it is becoming increasingly evident that the present competition between late capitalism and state socialism both suffer from a loss of a subject empowering praxis for the sake of bureaucratic techniques of control and manipulation. Why? There are many cognitive, epistemological, and socio-cultural reasons for this eclipse of subject empowerment in both macro-economic sys-tems. But there are also specifically metaphysical or ontological reasons. Justice is intrinsically universal in its claims on the con-science of humankind. Similar to the practice of reason, anything less than universally valid claims is a retreat into obscurantism and barbarism. The subject-empowering desires for justice and for reason are desires which concretely and dialectically transcend the limitations of this or that particular time, this or that particular place. The millions upon millions of the dead and the yet unborn, the species-being of humankind stretching back into the distances of the past and the unknowns of the future, cannot be excommunicated from the claims of justice and of reason. To do this is to isolate both our own present consciousness and our own present conscience in a solipsistic subjectivity which lies at the basis of both capitalist privatism and communist collectivism. The genuine species-being of humankind on this planet can only be appropriated and realized in praxis if the utopian efforts for justice and reason are ultimately validated and redeemed by the Mysterious Presence of God as Infinite Intelligence, Love, and empowering Freedom. The dead, especially the innocent victims of domination, stake a claim in their past histories of suffering for redemptive justification. In this context, which has been articulated in much greater detail by Helmut Peukert, the claims of reason for justice are sublated into the prayers and praxis of Christian faith.[25] This sublation is anything but a passive, merely contemplative, resignation in the face of contemporary injustice and domination. It is rather the inspiration which alone can make fully reasonable and responsible the praxis of justice. For the metaphysical or ontological reality of God empowering us to be subjects of our species' history is precisely the Inter-Subjective Presence which guarantees that praxis remains praxis. Otherwise our efforts confront, not Inter-Subjective Presence, but the merely objective expanses of space and time as things to be controlled and manipulated as best they can by cosmic orphans, whose ontological fear and insecurity make mockery of justice and reason. Such metaphysical contradictions inherent in a secularist basis of society breed the dehumanizing and unjust techniques of empire and superpower building. The tragic transitions from pre-modern sacralisms to modern secularisms, which left unchallenged so many forms of domination and control, dare not be repeated in the post-modern period we are now entering. Political and liberation theologies, and the movements of which they are part, are struggling to provide creative, free, and just new social orders dialectically attentive to the dangers of both sacralism and secularism.

NOTES

1. Cf. his *Theology of The World* (New York: Herder & Herder, 1969), pp. 98ff; also his *Glaube in Geschichte und Gesellschaft* (Mainz: Grünewald Verlag, 1977), pp. 38ff.

2. *Ibid.* pp. 166f.

3. I use the designation of "technocentrism" rather than the terms of "homocentrism" or "androcentrism" since technocentrism is the ecological form these latter take; cf. Rosemary Ruether, *Liberation Theology* (New York: Paulist Press, 1972), pp. 115–26; also her *Sexism and God-Talk* (Boston: Beacon Press, 1983), pp. 263–66.

4. Cf. his *A Theology of Liberation* (Maryknoll: Orbis Books, 1973), p. 5.

5. Cf. his *The Liberation of Theology* (Maryknoll: Orbis Books, 1976), p. 40.

6. Cf. his *Prophecy Deliverance* (Philadelphia: Westminster Press, 1982), pp. 15, 96ff.

7. Cf. Rosemary Ruether, *Liberation Theology;* Letty Russell, *Human Liberation in a Feminist Perspective* (Philadelphia: Westminster, 1974), pp. 50ff.

8. Cf. Charles Birch and John Cobb, *The Liberation of Life* (London: Cambridge University Press, 1981), pp 84ff.

9. Cf. his *Método para una filosofía de la liberación* (Salamanca: Sigueme, 1974).

10. Cf. his *Process Theology as Political Theology* (Philadelphia: Westminster Press, 1982); also his co-authored book with C. Birch, *The Liberation of Life,* pp. 85ff.

11. Care is called for in discussing "post-modern" contexts. Cf. Gutierrez, *The Power of the Poor in History* (Maryknoll: Orbis, 1983), p. 213.

12. Cf. her *Liberation Theology,* pp. 2–3.

13. On the theological criticisms of liberation theology, cf. among others Michael Novak (ed.), *Liberation South, Liberation North* (Washington, D.C.: American Enterprise Institute, 1981); Dennis McCann, *Christian Realism and Liberation Theology* (Maryknoll: Orbis Books, 1981); Darrol Bryant, "Should Sin Be Politicized?" in *The Ecumenist,* Vol. 21, No. 4 (May–June, 1983), pp. 49–54. On post-Christian criticisms of feminist liberation theology, cf. Mary Daly, *Gyn/Ecology: The Metaethics of Radical Feminism* (Boston: Beacon Press, 1978); Naomi Goldenberg, *Changing of the Gods* (Boston: Beacon Press, 1979); in Latin America Althusserian Marxism is some-

times invoked to argue for a basic contradiction in the project of liberation theology.

14. For Marx's discussion of these two phases or sets of methods, cf. his "Introduction" to *Grundrisse: Foundations of the Critique of Political Economy,* trans. by M. Nicolaus (New York: Vintage, 1973), pp. 100ff; also his "Author's Preface" or "Afterword" to the 2nd German edition of *Capital,* Vol. 1, ed. by F. Engels (New York: International Publishers, 1967), pp. 12–20. For an excellent study of this twofold approach, cf. Joseph O'Malley, "Marx, Marxism and Method" in S. Avineri (ed.), *The Varieties of Marxism* (The Hague: Nijhof, 1977), pp. 7–41.

15. For a more detailed exposition, cf. the article of Joseph O'Malley referred to above.

16. *The Poverty of Philosophy* in Vol. 6 of the *Collected Works* (New York: International Publishers, 1976), p. 163.

17. G. Baum, *Religion and Alienation* (New York: Paulist, 1975), p. 33.

18. Cf. Herder's *Reflections on the Philosophy of the History of Mankind,* trans. by Frank Manuel (Chicago: University of Chicago Press, 1968), p. 320

19. Cf. C. Taylor, *Hegel* (New York: Cambridge University Press, 1975), pp. 13ff.

20. *Ibid.,* pp. 389–571.

21. L. Feuerbach, *Das Wesen des Christentums,* ed. A. Esser (Köln: Verlag Jacob Hegner, 1967), p. 113.

22. Marx's fourth thesis on Feuerbach.

23. Habermas, as yet unpublished lecture on modernity, Boston University, 1983.

24. Cf. my "Christianity Within the Political Dialectics of Community and Empire," in *Method: A Journal of Lonergan Studies,* Vol. 1, No. 1 (Spring 1983), pp. 1–30; also my "Die Dialektik von Theorie und Praxis in der Paradigmenanalyse" in Hans Küng, ed., *Ein Neues Paradigma von der Theologie?* (Zürich: Benziger, 1984).

25. Cf. his *Science—Action—Fundamental Theology* (Boston: M.I.T. Press, 1984), pp. 216–275.

Douglas John Hall

Theology Is an Earth Science

INTRODUCTION

As during other great transitional periods in its historical pilgrim-age, so today—and perhaps more dramatically than ever before—the Church is torn between faithfulness to its traditions and prophetic vigilance in its social context. In the West this struggle is evident in both Protestant and Catholic circles. Significant minorities in both historic branches of Christianity, sensing the critical nature of our historical moment, insist that the Gospel was intended for humankind and that therefore the tradition must undergo whatever alterations are necessary for the witness-ing community genuinely to engage the human condition. This in turn—predictably enough, for the student of ecclesias-tical history—begets reactions from guardians of tradition, who fear that an anthropocentric focus is undermining the theocentrism of Christian truth, and that the faith will lose itself in humanism.

In this essay honoring one who, especially in the North American context, has been at the center of this struggle, I wish to articulate a brief but, I hope, basic response to the issues at stake in it. As my title already and perhaps too blatantly implies, my sympathies lie with those who think it the Christian mandate to fashion a theology and a gospel that addresses the human sit-uation. At the same time—and in this I feel a rudimentary kin-ship with Professor Baum—I do not see why what is truest and best in our tradition cannot serve precisely that end.

1. THE DANGERS OF A CONSERVATIVE APPROACH TO THE PAST

All Christian theology involves reflection upon the past, notably upon those "core events" which constitute the rudimentary data of constructive theology, but also upon the doctrinal constellations of past theological discourse which have grouped themselves around the ongoing contemplation of those same events. It would not be *Christian* theology apart from this reflection upon its own formative past. What is called systematic or dogmatic theology is therefore always in part historical theology.

There are however two quite different ways of regarding our past. One way conceives of the past articulation of belief as something to be *preserved:* precious truth which must not be overlooked or superseded or demeaned.[1] In practice, of course, this has normally meant loyalty to some particular expression of Christian belief—for example to a distinctive doctrinal tradition such as that of Thomas or Calvin or the early ecumenical councils. It would after all be difficult if not impossible to set oneself up as conserver of *everything* that could legitimately be claimed as Christian tradition. Even when what is to be preserved is stated in very general terms ("the truth of Scripture," "apostolic tradition," "Reformation theology," etc.) it is usually some rather circumscribed *interpretation* of the thing in question that is meant. For while (e.g.) "Reformation theology" obviously delineates a particular area of historical concentration, every student of the sixteenth century knows that there are vast differences between the various expressions of faith that eventually gathered themselves together under the aegis of "the Reformation." Thus a danger perennially associated with the preservative approach to the past is indicated as soon as one asks (and someone inevitably does ask): Which past, and interpreted by whom?

Regardless of this obvious limitation, the conserving attitude toward the Christian past has played, and still plays, a highly significant role in the life of the Church. It is at least possible, in fact, that this type of orientation has been normative for most professional theology. I do not refer to the "giants" of our almost two thousand year old tradition, whose prominence is due largely to the fact that they *broke* with their past, i.e., with the regnant doctrinal conventions of their times, having sensed new questions to which those conventions could not speak. I refer rather to the myriad generations of theological teachers at every level of pedagogy in the Church who, on account of the less critical spirit of their ages or because they lacked insight or courage, did not think the faith in an original way but conceived of their task as the husbanding of established dogma. Often in our enthusiasm for the twenty or thirty names that are writ large in Christian intellectual history we fail to recognize that the spirit of professional theology has been shaped less by the Bachs and Mozarts of our discipline than by the generations of practitioners who, like local piano teachers, thought it their duty to transmit intact the creations of the great ones. Combined as this has been since the Great Schism, and in the West since the Reformation, with ecclesiastical fragmentation and denominationalism, it has resulted in a veritable plethora of tradition*alisms* from which it is very difficult for the Church to extricate itself. Thus a second danger associated with the conserving attitude toward the Christian past is the barrier that it presents to ecumenical discourse. This barrier has long been experienced as a frustration; but in a time like our own, when global issues of immense proportions threaten the very life of the planet, it must be regarded as a real danger. For surely it is a mark of extreme disobedience to the Lord and Giver of *life* when theological groupings are so preoccupied with their faithfulness to this or that (often truncated) past that they are prevented from engaging in a wholehearted and corporate exploration of the meaning of Christian hope for the present and the future.

Let me pause long enough at this point to explore some of its nuances and implications. I think that it is hard to overestimate the influence upon the entire Christian movement of entrenched forms of doctrinalism. During the second half of the present Century, to be sure, we have seen the development of some significant experiments in 'ecumenical' theology—that is, in expressions of Christian belief which are ready to range very widely within the total tradition for the meaning of faith. Some of these experiments have proven unusually successful in transcending dogmatic and denomination loyalties.[2] It might even be claimed that the most gripping and "original" expressions of Christian theology in our epoch have all, one way or another, set aside the ingrained habit of protecting their own credal traditions and opened themselves anew to the great variety that is the Christian theological past. Yet, while this generalization could be sustained by comparison with past forms of narrow doctrinal isolationism, by comparison with our *potential* for ecumenical theological reflection—and the overwhelming need for it—our ecclesiastical performance is certainly less than impressive. For all our ecumenical "contact" at the practical level, the great majority of Western Christians, including professional theologians, are still more comfortable in the various dogmatic niches into which we were born or in which we were trained. This is borne out by the fact that while there are today interesting centers of ecumenical theological education, the churches still evince an unusual commitment to the denominational seminary. Even where sheer parochialism has given way to "clusters" of denominational schools, membership in these amalgams consists chiefly of more or less compatible confessional groupings; moreover, anyone who knows something of the interior life of such institutions is well aware that ecumenical arrangements at the organizational level do not automatically result in inter-confessional, let alone genuinely ecumenical, dialogue. Besides, whole branches of the *Oekumene* remain fundamental strangers to one another. In the West, the religious and theological milieu of Eastern Orthodoxy is as remote from the minds of most theological students and teachers as are the mysteries of Zoroastrianism. In sum, for the majority within the professional theological community of the universal Church, "doing theology" still means working within the basic parameters of quite explicit and circumscribed doctrinal traditions. The past—or rather our way of living with it—still sways the present.

Insofar as this assessment is true, it is alarming enough in itself; but unfortunately this ecclesial failure sufficiently to transcend our various pasts is combined today with a sociological factor that makes it even more alarming. Suppose we grant that important strides toward a more genuinely "catholic" approach to Christian theology have indeed been made. Suppose that there is an increasing openness to the beliefs and traditions of "the others" and not just a bourgeois friendliness. Suppose that more and more of the "young blood" entering the lists of professional theology, having fewer strong denominational ties and less fixed dogmatic loyalties, are in fact ready to recognize truth wherever they may find it. This still does not guarantee the emergence of a different attitude toward the past as such. Most of us who work in institutions of theological education realize, for one thing, that among those who turn to the study of this discipline in our apocalyptic times there are significant numbers who do so out of a psychic need to embrace a past that can insulate them from the cold winds of the present and the future. There may be, even, a greater pull toward the past-as-end today than in earlier periods, despite the lessening of a priori commitment to explicit dogmatic conventions. Understandable as this may be (for it is somehow a sign of incipient sanity to wish to escape from what is in many respects an insane world), it means that the dangers of the presserving attitude toward our doctrinal past are by no means passé. Indeed, the "conservative" element that has become increasingly powerful in all of our churches, especially on this continent, would suggest that a new or at least an intensified danger has been added to the two that we have already adduced as being inherent in the preservative mentality. I refer of course to its appeal to escapism—an appeal which, as Marx reminded us, seems endemic with religion, but one which is doubly alluring under the conditions of "future shock."

2. THE SEARCH FOR "A USABLE PAST"

When the past, or some aspect of it, is regarded as the locus of ultimate truth, theology is quite consistently equated with the profession of a credal posture based upon that past. The task of the theological community is then seen as the articulate and persuasive enunciation of this credo in church and society. The basic content of the Christian "message" is derived quite independently of the present context of those who "announce" it. It is a matter of truth already "given": given in Scripture, in the corporate memory of the Church, in the historic decisions of councils, etc. The responsibility of theology is to acquaint itself with and reflect upon this givenness, under the guidance of the divine Spirit, and to search for the most auspicious ways of communicating it.

In contrast to this preserving attitude toward the past, the second way of regarding our Christian sources and resources is inspired chiefly by the need to meet, comprehend, and address the present. One searches for "a usable past" (Martin Marty). This is not a merely utilitarian attitude toward Christian tradition, any more than the formerly discussed position is *merely* antiquarian. Turning to the past for *help* is after all a very concrete way of honoring our past. Could we, who work as theologians today, desire of future communities of faith anything more gratifying than that they should think of returning to us, occasionally, for assistance in making *their own* confession of trust? Surely we would incur certain scriptural censure if, beyond that, we desired that they uphold *our* witness as if it were sufficient also for their situation. Interest in the past for its own sake may be commendable in the historian, but the theologian works within a framework of existential need—namely, the Church. The Church needs to discover, always afresh, what it believes and how it can address the world around it and within it. It needs to find light for the real darkness of that real world. It needs, in short, *to confess the faith.*

Note the *con*fession of the faith is quite distinct from faith's *pro*fession, no matter how inextricably the two acts may be related. Confession, as the term itself suggests, means to stand *with, alongside,* and *in* one's historical moment and to meet the specific possibilities and impossibilities of that moment as a Christian witness to the grace and hope being revealed in the Christ. Professing the faith is no substitute for confessing it, and while the preserving approach to the past may be able to serve faith's profession it does not serve faith's confession. I may know all the creeds, catechisms, formulae, systems, doctrines, dogmas, soteriological principles and scriptures of the tradition and be able impressively to cite and recite them; but if I am ignorant of or detached from the concrete realities of my world—realities containing new questions to which the wisdom of the past cannot speak directly—then all my professional aptitude will be as sounding brass and tinkling cymbal. Or, as one of the aforementioned "giants" of the tradition of Jerusalem has stated the matter with characteristic and colorful directness:

> If I profess with the loudest voice and clearest exposition every portion of the truth of God except precisely that little point which the world and the devil are at that moment attacking, I am not *confessing* Christ, however boldly I may be *professing* him. Where the battle ranges, there the loyalty of the soldier is tested, and to be steady on all the battlefield besides is mere flight and disgrace if he flinches at that point.[3]

The distinction between confession and profession will not be fully appreciated until it is understood that it is possible for Christians not only to substitute profession of the faith for faith's confession, but that professing Christ may (and regularly does) become a way of *avoiding* confession. An illustration from recent history will aid in establishing the point: During the 1930's, Heinrich Grüber, dean of the Berlin Cathedral and founder of the so-called *Grüber-Büro,* which assisted Jews in escaping from Nazi Germany, announced: "To preach the *gospel* now means to proclaim that Jesus Christ was a Jew." The *wisdom* (not only the courage) of this statement can only be grasped at the imiginative level if it is juxtaposed with a contemporary pronouncement— one offered by the so-called *Reichsbischof,* Ludwig Müller, Hitler's friend and personal appointment. When challenged about his orthodoxy, Müller calmly stated: "I believe *all* the creeds."

The confessional posture does not despise the need of the Christian community for a "professional" awareness of its rich and varied credal and doctrinal past. In chastising those who substitute profession for confession, Luther, the "professor of theology," was certainly not suggesting that the professional dimension of the theological task be abandoned. He was only insisting, as he did in many other ways, that the profession of the faith is a means to its confession. The past must be struggled with, and in a very professional manner. But the goal of this struggle is not the preservation of the past; it is the preservation of present and future, that is, the preservation of life against all that would annihilate it. Ludwig Müller used his professional knowledge of the tradition as a means of avoiding confession—a fence to sit upon. He was of course not alone in that historical cauldron, where real confession *(mārtus)* could so easily lead to literal martyrdom. Grüber on the other hand used his professional awareness of the tradition to help him discover just the appropriate formulation, the prophetic "word from the Lord," in short the "gospel" that could truly *engage* "the little point . . . where the battle rages."

3. CONVERSION TO THE WORLD

It seems probable that the two different ways of regarding our Christian past are aspects of two conceptions of faith and theology as a whole, more particularly of their relation to life in this world. If worldly life matters in some ultimate sense, then faith and theology cannot settle for profession but are driven continuously toward a confessional encounter with "the world and the devil" (Luther). If on the other hand this world and its destiny are not part of what faith conceives to be its "ultimate concern" (Tillich), if on the contrary ultimacy is pictured in terms wholly or mainly transcendent of historical existence, then the *pro*fession of the faith amid the vicissitudes of worldly life can itself and as such be thought the only *con*fession in which the religious community is interested. But the questions is: Given the particularities of our tradition, especially of the "core events" testified to by the Scriptures of the older and newer Testaments, how could it be thought within the sphere of such a faith that this world and its destiny do *not* matter, and ultimately so?

It is of course true that the "modest science" (Barth) of theology, like every other science, has its own internal fascination. It can be enormously exhilarating—at least as absorbing as a chess game or a problem in theoretical mathematics—to devote one's intelligence to the contemplation of the linguistic symbols associated with trinitarian thought concerning the Deity, or to observe great minds like Origen's and Occam's being drawn by their own inexorable logic to strange conclusions abhorrent, often enough, to their own souls. Yet it surely represents a transgression of the basic data of *this* science when its practitioners become so preoccupied with the internal dynamics of their discipline that they grow oblivious to the world. Do not the internal dynamics of this science in fact lead one, even against one's will, straight to the heart of this world's darkness—and its overcoming? The atonement, the terrible questions of divine sovereignty and election, the Trinity itself—how could anyone seriously contemplate such mysteries without being driven mercilessly *toward* this world—toward the particular, "the neighbor"? To consider the one word only—"God"—as this word must be heard by any who are acquainted with the tradition of Jerusalem is surely to expose oneself in the most radical way to this world. As a child of the covenant has put it succinctly, "The way is no less important than the goal. He who thinks about God, forgetting man, runs the risk of mistaking his goal: God may be your next door neighbor."[4] That empirical Christianity has busied itself with doctrine in such a way as to avoid "the neighbor," the world, and with fearsome regularity, is indisputable. But despite the historical and psychological explanations that can be and have been offered, it remains a mystery how a faith so consistently orientated toward creation in its most original expressions could have produced religious and theological communities so consistently ambiguous in their attitude toward this world.

What therefore seems to me especially hopeful in Christian theology today is that many of those most active in the struggle to rethink the faith in the post-modern epoch have become conscious of precisely this incongruity. What unites movements as diverse as the various theologies of liberation, political theologies, feminist theologies, theologies of hope and of resistance, theologies of the cross and of "the pain of God,"[5] etc., is their common commitment to a gospel which has for its object the *shalom* of this world.

This "conversion to the world," as it may appropriately be designated, drives quite naturally to a new and profound interest on the part of Christians in the specifics of their times and places (theological contextuality), and to a confessionality whose object is change and not merely comprehension.[6] One observes in these emphases a revived appreciation of theological liberalism, and especially of the social gospel movement. Yet there is here a consciousness of "the darker side" that our liberal forebears did not and perhaps could not know: the world, for our generations, does not move inevitably toward the Light. The vulnerability of creation is a given of contemporary experience. But in contrast to earlier forms of religious consciousness of the perilous character of finitude, this recognition has not led the theologians who are perhaps most sensitive to it toward a posture of earthly resignation and a flight to the eternal. Dietrich Bonhoeffer already spoke for many post-war Christian thinkers when, over against the profession of an otherworldly faith, he wrote:

> In Christ we are offered the possibility of partaking in the reality of God and in the reality of the world, but not in the one without the other. The reality of God discloses itself only by setting me entirely in the reality of the world, and when I encounter the reality of the world it is always already sustained, accepted and reconciled in the reality of God. This is the inner meaning of the revelation of God in the man Jesus Christ.[7]

Like Bonhoeffer—a German intellectual of higher bourgeois background, who two generations earlier might have been claimed for secular humanism—a significant minority of our contemporaries have been drawn to biblical faith precisely because they perceive in it an ultimate concern for humanity and all life which is at the same time deeply conscious of that which negates life. For such persons, the gods of modernity have failed; but the commitment to historical existence which inspired humanism from the Renaissance onward is still alive in them.

The humanistic background and bent of the cutting edge of theology resulting from the influence of such persons and movements ought not to surprise anyone. After all, humanism evolved out of the Judaeo-Christian tradition, and in its origins it is practically indistinguishable from the reforming movements of late medieval Christianity. If anything, the present "anthropocentric" influence upon mainstream Christianity is nothing but a consequence of the joyful return to the father's house of a prodigal who left home with treasures belonging to the household but dreams of autonomy, and has come back in a mood of chastened realism and sober hope. That dimension of the Renaissance which was not swallowed up in technocratic delusion but retained something of the humanistic commitment to the *being* of homo sapiens which transcends the creature's *making* and *doing* has in some tangible sense rejoined itself to the household of faith. Or, if it is too optimistic to speak as though a full reconciliation had occurred (for many friends of humanity and the earth can still find no home in the Church), at least it is known, on both sides of this modern chasm between sacred and secular, that there are friends on the other side.

Part of what keeps the "friends" apart still is to be laid at the doorstep of the household of faith. For there is in that sphere— which was also impoverished by the departure of the prodigal humanists—an "elder brother" mentality that resists the homecoming of a disillusioned but still-committed humanism. In its departure from official Christianity, humanism took with it a large part of the inherent if unexplored Christian orientation toward this world and permitted, in a Church now much deprived of the humanistic impulse, the development of an ideological theocentrism. By ideological theocentrism I mean an exclusivistic concentration upon the divine which, while it obviously does not eliminate the human and historical from its purview, effectively reduces the latter to the status of the penultimate, at best, and impedes reciprocity between the eternal and time, grace and nature, heaven and earth. Ideological theocentrism is in other words a dimension of that separation of the sacred and the secular which occurred with the breakdown of medieval "theonomy" (Tillich). Retreating into the realm of the sacred, the Church, still heir to the dubious benefits of established religion, appropriated to its exclusive use and control "God and the things of God." Unlike biblical theocentrism, which incorporates the geocentric and anthropocentric thrust of prophetic faith into itself and therefore ranges widely in the world for intimations of transcendence, ideological theocentrism in its various manifestations maintains the strict independence and priority of divinely revealed truth, and authority structures appropriate to the same.

What we have been witnessing, I believe, in both Protestant and Catholic spheres of thought and life, is an attempt on the part of persons and movements that for a variety of reasons have been "converted to the world" to reclaim and rethink for Christian faith *in God* the vigilance for humanity and the biosphere which belongs to the oldest and deepest strata of biblical theocentrism. If this attempt is experienced by the guardians of reputed orthodoxies as a capitulation to humanism; if those who seek to comprehend and to change the world are accused of anthropocentrism; if theologians and Christian activists who strive to engage a world on the brink of multifold disaster are taunted with confusing theology and sociology, faith and politics, then the guardians must be invited to consider again these oldest and deepest sources of the tradition they claim to defend; for those sources testify only to a God who will to be *our* God, to be Emmanuel.

CONCLUSION

Theology, as distinguished from the history of dogma, must always be orientated toward confessional address. It must itself *be* address, and it must equip the whole Church to address its worldly context. No Christian theologian is at liberty to formulate this address arbitrarily, or with a one-sided concern for its immediate "relevance." The science of theology absolutely demands an ongoing dialogue with its own past.

But this dialogue is not at all, for the theologian, an end in itself. In the Church there will always be a place for the intelligent and trained profession of Christian doctrine; more than that, the studied reflection of what has been "handed over" *(tradere)* to us will demand more, not less, professional competence the more the Christian movement pursues a truly ecumenical path. The breadth and depth—and the sheer volume—of doctrinal material accumulated over twenty centuries, if taken seriously, requires an ongoing and disciplined study if it is to yield the "help" that we need from it. It also contains enough puzzles, contradictions, and lacunae to make all of us sympathetic with Karl Barth's half-whimsical hope that he might, after listening to Mozart, be granted long discourse in heaven with Calvin and Schleiermacher.

Yes—in heaven! But theology is an earth science. It exists for the Church, which exists for the world. It is (as Barth too insisted) finally not a theoretical but a practical science. It knows, that is to say, that it must try to help the human race avoid the "death" with which it is always making wayward covenant (Isaiah 28) and discover the "abundant life" that it is always being offered. This is its guiding methodological principle, imposed upon it by the incarnate, crucified and risen Word at its center. Nothing therefore out of the past, no matter how curious or beautiful in itself, can command the position of primacy in this earth science. Eternity itself, so far as this science is concerned, exists for time, just as that poignant symbol of eternal rest, the sabbath, exists for humankind, and not the other way around.

Because the eternal is always breaking into time, forever seeking communion with the creatures of time, no time is uninteresting to theology. On that premise, one may expect to be rewarded for any disciplined reflection upon time past. It is not necessary to belittle tradition in the name of ultimate concern for the *hic et nunc.* Yet the incarnational commitment to creation carries with it, with an unrelenting logic, abiding and intensive vigilance for the present—including what we call future, that yet undecided and open end of the present. Therefore while I shall, with Barth, be happy to discourse for light years with all the great ones of our past, seated upon some grassy knoll in Paradise, my earthly vocation prevents me from tarrying with them for their own sakes. Like a confused but perhaps maturing adolescent improvising his way in a world grown poor in truth, I shall go to these fathers and mothers in the faith chiefly for help and encouragement. And I suspect that they, good parents, will quite understand my reluctance to remain with them any longer than necessary.

NOTES

1. The preserving or conserving attitude toward the past is usually linked with a propositional or conceptual attitude toward revelation— what Professor Lindbeck of Yale in his new and important study, *The Nature of Doctrine* (Philadelphia, Westminster Press, 1984), calls the "pre-liberal propositionalist" theory of religion and doctrine.

2. In North America no one has been more imaginative and courageous in precisely this venture than Gregory Baum. Not only has he opened himself in an exceptional way to the many shadings of Protestant*ism,* he has made himself personally accessible to many Protestants, again and again crossing over the often sacrosanct boundaries that Christians have erected and maintained over centuries as if they were only half real—which is probably the only reasonable way to regard them.

3. In my "The Diversity of Christian Witnessing in the Tension Between Subjection to the Word and Relation to the Context," in *Luther's Ecumenical Significance*, Peter Manns and Harding Meyer, eds. (Philadelphia: Fortress Press, 1984), pp. 247-268.

4. Elie Wiesel, *The Town Beyond the Wall* (N.Y.: Schocken Books, 1982), p. 115

5. I am thinking here not only of the work of Moltmann and other Western theologians who pursue the *theologia crucis,* but also of Eastern thinkers like Kosuke Koyama (e.g., *Mount Fuji and Mount Sinai: A Pilgrimage in Theology* (London: S. C. M. Press, 1984), C S. Song (e.g., *The Compassionate God* (Maryknoll: Orbis Books, 1982) and others, many of whom are influenced by Kitamori's "theology of the pain of God."

6. Cf. Rosemary Radford Ruether, *To Change the World: Christology and Cultural Criticism* (London: S. C. M. Press, 1981).

7. Cf. Dietrich Bonhoeffer, *Ethics,* edited by Eberhard Bethge (New York: Macmillan, 1965).

Dorothee Sölle

Peace Needs Women

I recently got two newspaper clippings on the subject of armaments: one of them reports that President Reagan and his three
closest associates have taken a wonderful, fascinating flight in a
jumbo jet called "Doomsday" which was designed for the case of
a nuclear war. Reagan was deeply impressed and said, "It gives
me a feeling of confidence!" (*Boston Globe,* November 16, 1981).
The other article deals with the scientific council of the Defense
Department which recommends the delivery of new nerve gas to
England. A woman scientist in the Pentagon reports about the
plans for a new colorless, odorless gas which causes vomiting and
cramps, resulting in death in a few minutes (*Frankfurter Rund-
schau,* December 29, 1981).

When I compare these two news items, I realize that a minor
detail disturbs me deeply: that it is a woman who speaks for the
Pentagon and wants this gas tested. I didn't expect anything from
Ronald Reagan other than this joy in a complicated modern mur-
der instrument, but that in the scientific council of the Defense
Department a woman is preparing chemical warfare—I cannot
grasp it. Am I so naive that I think of all women first as sisters?
Or conservative, since I immediately try to picture Amoretta
Hoeber as the mother of two sweet children? I read the second
news item three times, in hopes of finding a typographical error
and perhaps determining that it was actually a man after all.

The theme women and peace touches me not only on a rational level; it connects with deep hopes with which I live, and the
news about this woman working in the mightiest death machine
in the world insults my hopes. "Dear Amoretta," I would like to
write in a letter, "do you really know what you are doing? And

for whom you are preparing something? Don't you believe that this thing you're working on from 9 to 5, and may now even publicly promote, will affect your children too? That the quality of their lives will be different, if all the billion dollar projects which you publicly advocate are realized? Aren't you afraid that the next despairing unemployed youth in Washington could beat up your son? Haven't you ever thought about the question what science really is, and whether what you are doing really falls into that category? What are you using your intelligence for? In whose interest are you working, dear Amoretta—after all, you're a woman! That does imply a certain dignity! I certainly can't imagine that you would sell your body by going to bed with someone for money. But you want to sell your new nerve gas bombs to the Western world. You want to try them out in a test area in the state of Utah and stockpile masses of them in Great Britain for a chemical war in Europe. That is your recommendation, Amoretta, and I still can't comprehend it."

It's very difficult for me to separate women and peace. By this I mean the following: as a man you can realize yourself in war. As far back as we know of, men have realized themselves in war; there they have found their identity, their name or epaulets to replace a name, their adventure, their life involvement, in short, themselves.

At the beginning of our culture stands a great epic which essentially deals with war, slaughter, military campaigns, conquest, looting, rape, duels, blood, death—the *Iliad.* Even the men who can't take part in this epic Trojan war have found in it a cultural model for their identity. Human being equals man and man equals hero—and this is all realized in war, the great rite of passage.

Women's part in this great epic poem is peace, the home, the farm, the olive trees. This means that for their—very limited—self-realization, women need peace.

A woman can't become a human being through, with and for war. You can become a "hyena of the battlefield," like Brecht's Mother Courage, you can imagine you're making a profit from war, but you can't become a human being in this way. You can only become a mother against war, not with it, as Brecht convincingly portrayed: whenever Courage strikes a bargain and tries to reorganize herself economically through war, that is always when she loses one of her children. These two roles—to be there for war and to be there for the children—simply don't go together. I'd like to apply to our own situation, which is very different both historically and in regard to class, what I've learned from "Mother Courage." Amoretta Hoeber, scientist at the Pentagon, cannot promote nuclear war and at the same time become a female human being.

But this contradiction is in each of us; if we pay taxes to prepare for war, if we are trained by and planned into the health care system "in case of defense," or even, as women, join the military when not enough male soldiers are available, these activities contradict what it means to become a woman, a human being. All of these activities are directly related to the nuclear holocaust appearing on the horizon.

Here I would like to throw in a basic reflection which presents a kind of "feminist reading of the Bible." By this I mean an exegesis of the Bible which does not follow the standards and interests of the large churches and their hierarchy, but a new way of understanding the Bible which has grown up out of Christian women's groups.

Many people know the mythical tale of the oldest couple, Adam and Eve. Here I am dealing with the story of their two children Cain and Abel. Cain was a farmer, who brought God an offering from the fruits of the field. Abel was a shepherd, who brought an offering from the firstlings of his flock. But the Lord looks "graciously" only on the offering of the one; according to the story, Cain's offering displeased him. Cain becomes furious and his gestures are distorted. I want to cite now what happens then, to make clear how it was at the beginning and still is today.

"And when they were in the field, Cain rose up against his brother Abel, and killed him. Then the Lord said to Cain, 'Where is Abel your brother?' He said, 'I do not know; am I my brother's keeper?' And the Lord said, 'What have you done? The voice of your brother's blood is crying to me from the ground'" (Gen 4:8-10).

This old story sums up what I want to call the basic fact of our culture: that the C-group kills the A-group. It happens every day and it is being told, filmed and pushed; the story of Cain and Abel is constantly becoming technologically improved and psychologically deeper. Its anthropological presupposition is: the two human possibilities are Cain and Abel, executioner or victim. Do wrong or suffer wrong, as Socrates said. Be number one, as Ronald Reagan emphasizes, as Cain in fact was, the first-born, or be number two. The first thing our children learn is to win (Cain) or to lose (Abel). Nuclear first-strike and the first-strike mentality are what we have chosen as guarantee for our survival. Better Cain than Abel.

In this tradition, the two human possibilities are Cain or Abel. The culture in which we live is Cain's culture. According to the Bible, Cain looks sullen, hates himself, and finally flees from himself into the city. The countryside is not his thing. "When you till the ground, it shall no longer yield to you its strength; you shall be a fugitive and a wanderer on the earth."

The earth itself is disturbed by the blood that was spilled, as if she already knew what Cain's descendants would do with it.

I spent several years of my adult life speaking for Abel and against Cain. For the powerless, whose blood still cries out, and against the gang of unfortunate C-people. For Abel and against the Lord Father who runs the whole show. A theology of pain and rage. The theology of one who is by nature second class, made out of the rib. But I don't read this story anymore with Abel's eyes. I am tired of being the blood, the earth and the scream. I address the storyteller and those who have passed the tale down, written it down, recited and believed it. Is that all? I ask the storyteller. Where am I then? Do I have to be Abel if I don't want to be Cain? Is there no other way?

Didn't Adam and Eve have any other children? I ask the storyteller. Did they only have sons?

The book from which this story comes is a document of patriarchy. Daughters and women belong to the category of objects which can be possessed. In relation to this story, it is superfluous to mention them. They have nothing to do with the matter. When women are killed, child-sacrifices made, no angel appears between the sacrificer and the victim.

Within the framework of this tradition, women are essentially invisible; as actors or victims they simply don't appear here.

I now correct my opening statement and say: man's possibilities are, according to this tradition, Cain or Abel. This is not an anti-male sentence: we can always find one whom we'd like to call Abel. If Cain was the sexist, who hates himself, is violent, distorts his face, then Abel was the gentle, feminist man, the flute player. But is it a feminist thesis, which criticizes the tradition and raises questions like: Is it possible to propose a human history "cleansed of women" as Hitler tried to "cleanse Europe of the Jews"? Can anything other than what we have here come from a myth which shares a sexist premise, namely that human being equals man? Can such a myth lead to more than the alternative Cain or Abel?

The word "fratricide" is current: is there also such a thing as sororicide? Not in our language, in any case. As long as we imagine God as a man, because we think of human beings as men, the story of the A-people and the C-people will continue. The God who rejected Cain's offering and who stands for Cain's self-hatred can neither punish nor forgive him. It is a story with no return, with no reconciliation. Cain goes into the cities—he has not changed. "Cain said to the Lord, 'My punishment is greater than I can bear. Behold, thou has driven me this day away from the ground; and from thy face I shall be hidden; and I shall be a fugitive and a wanderer on the earth, and whoever finds me will slay me.' Then the Lord said to him, 'Not so! If anyone slays Cain, vengeance shall be taken on him sevenfold.' And the Lord put a mark on Cain, lest any who came upon him should kill him."

The God of this story can do nothing for him; he makes him untouchable. In other words: the killing goes on. the possibilities of this God are exhausted in the model of the two men in this story, the man Cain and the man Abel. Where could hope come from there?

As long as human being is identified with man; as long as the human children who are mentioned are only sons; as long as God is masculine and not more than that; as long as the myth is silent about half of humanity; as long as brothers grow up not knowing what sisterhood is—so long will it continue to be just the way the story tells it: Abel's blood screams and Cain flies through space for militaristic purposes, unsettled and incapable of solving even one problem of the earth and its hungry children.

Did Adam and Eve have no other children? And how might the story be told anew? ˙

Given the presuppositions of our culture, which is a men's culture, nothing can change. Peace needs other people, and other forms of behavior, than those which have developed so far. Peace—if we mean more by the word than the occasional absence of war—needs women.

I don't mean that women are more peaceful or better. I don't even know if their inhibitions agaist killing are stronger than those of men. But I do know that women are oppressed, at least in the societies which are relevant to us. Disadvantaged, exploited, raped—and one of the means by which this has happened and happens is war. Although of course it's not called that anymore. Today we call the method by which women in particular are disadvantaged, exploited and subjected to violence, "defense"; the higher value which goes with it is called "security." That is a propaganda word which sounds attractive, warm and comforting, especially in the ears of those who experience less social peace. Women are lured into the trap of the "promise of security" because they are economically and psychologically so insecure. On account of their sex they are not hired, are more easily fired and worse paid. By the use of the word "security"— which sounds social but means something entirely military— women, above all, women, are lied to about the actual mutual armed threats, and tricked out of the quality of life which they need for themselves and their children. By quality of life I mean really simple things, like a safe way to bicycle to school, clean water, enough doctors, etc. Women are not more peaceful "by nature," if there is such a thing; it is only that war—by which I mean the one we are preparing for as well—hits them harder. On this point I agree completely with the government minister who is responsible for the preparation for nuclear war which is called "defense." He finds that women should also profit from "defense." "Why should only men receive a good education, while women in the army are generally employed in the kitchen, at the typewriter and with the dustrag?" He considers the voluntary enlistment of women (in non-combatant units, for the time being) to be a step toward equal rights for women.

One gets the strange impression that Hans Apel is concerned about women's liberation, as though he were concerned about the educational possibilities of young women and not about armaments! That is a complete distortion of the facts: women's opportunities for good schooling and vocational training are decreasing because government spending for education and social services is being cut. For the overwhelming majority of women, more "defense" means more burdens, impairments and difficulties. The daily violence against everyone who wants a peaceful ecological balance proves this.

Women are not more peaceful, but they are more oppressed than their men. Therefore they are the natural allies of all who struggle against war and militarism. "Frauen für Frieden" (women for peace) isn't only alliterative; it is almost trivial. What dark times are we living in when we must militantly emphasize the obvious?

It follows from our history of oppression that women and peace belong together. If women place themselves on the other side, like Amoretta Hoeber as a scientist, or when they, without any consciousness, find themselves on the other side, then they have turned their backs on the oppressed and thereby deny themselves. For it is the poor who are most oppressed by the West German military apparatus and its billions for armaments: the rich north is conducting an economic war against the poor south, where each day, according to the most conservative estimates, 15,000 people "fall." Every minute one child under two years old starves to death. I can't speak about women and peace without mentioning this reality of the war already happening now, on which our own wealth is based.

This war against the poor hits no one harder than the poorest of the poor, that is, the women of the third world. This is true economically and it is also true of the torture specialists. The sexual component plays a special role in the torture of women. The wish to humiliate and debase the victim, to destroy a woman, leads to specific methods of torture: rape, mostly only by officers; rape by four men at the same time. All these methods of tormenting people are practiced with the same reason that the people who are arming us give when they demand more billions for overkill: the security of the state, national security as a new political ideology. "Human beings must be tortured because the security of the state demands it," said General Pinochet in Chile. One may vary this sentence with confidence: "Human beings must starve because the security of the industrialized nations demands it."

Women are the natural allies of peace. If we forget that, if we turn our backs on the poorest of the poor, as in "It's great to have a husband who's in the army," then we have internalized the militarism which rules over us; we have made it into our own thing, adapted ourselves to the conceptions and values of the ruling men.

For a woman to become conscious of her situation means a break with the values on which we are raised, a break with the peacelessness with which we have been vaccinated. Militarism, use of violence, permanent preparation to exterminate others with a fist, is one of the central values of partriarchy. To become a woman means to become a woman for peace.

The way there is scary; deviation from "what is done," dissent, standing alone, causes special difficulties for women who are brought up to compromise and harmonize. I want to start with my own experience, which goes back to the time of rearmament of West Germany. For me, who grew up in a city which was burned out and bombed to rubble, it was incredible that in this Germany, which had begun and lost two world wars, they were recruiting for the army again, that tanks and submarines were to be built again, that nuclear weapons were being stockpiled. This couldn't be true! This wasn't the will of the population! Had anybody asked these people what they wanted? But with this rage in my gut, with indignation at a politics which lied to people and parliament, I was suddenly very alone. The experiences of resistance against remilitarization were hard and bitter. "Loneliness" is a big word, but I'm thinking of the many little demonstrations and gatherings, thirty, maybe fifty people, long standing and thin singing, cold and no good shoes, a classroom in an elementary school, pathetic speeches, songs and poetry from the 1920's, when that had all happened already once before. We were alone, miserably alone; we were weak; peace had no lobby. It was less and less worth it for the press. I remember one thing about these meetings which recalls exactly the bitter taste in my mouth from that time, namely that at each of these demonstrations were a bunch of older women, with wrinkled faces, clear eyes and old-fashioned, shabby coats. These women were called "peace aunts" and this expression is very German and incredibly cynical, bringing together the political climate which dominates just as much today: sexism, "this is not worth taking seriously for there are so many women there," ageism, discrimination against older people, and just the arrogance of power. "Why bother with a bunch of peace aunts?" a smart young journalist said to me.

Well, why bother with them. It is one of the bitter experiences, to be alone with very few, together with the unsightly, the altogether wrong people. Not with fellow students, not with people from my neighborhood, not with my family, not even with people from my own social class. Since that time, loneliness is connected for me with a quality I find almost unbearable: it is ridiculous. It makes one ridiculous. "What are you doing there?" my mother said to me. "You're just making youself ridiculous." She was completely right.

Isolation cuts us off from each other, it weakens us, it destroys our potential for self-expression, isolation takes away courage and strength, but the basis of all is the ridicule to which one defenselessly exposes oneself. The fear of making oneself ridiculous is very deep-seated. To think and act in a deficient way, to be a dissident, means physical isolation—suddenly everyone is the other side; it means temporal isolation—you're really out-of-date; it means mental isolation—you haven't understood the constraints of the situation and the legal possibilities at all; but the worst thing is the emotional isolation—you're just making yourself ridiculous.

Most everyday experiences of isolation have to do with the fear of appearing ridiculous. If I, as a woman, go into a bar alone,

I really need very sturdy self-confidence to stand going in alone, ordering alone, paying alone. I haven't been brought up to do that—on the contrary. In my upbringing—and this is true of most women in my generation and social class—the fears of standing alone, of undertaking something on one's own, of behaving in a deviant way, are deeply rooted and connected with the fear of appearing ridiculous. Self-confidence, independence from the judgment of others, the ability to differentiate oneself, to resist, to go one's way alone, may perhaps belong to a boy's upbringing, but certainly not to that of a girl. A few weeks ago I was standing at the fruit stand. An older gentleman in front of me asked for oranges; the saleswoman said, "Here, very fresh, straight from South Africa." Earlier I had gotten information about the fruit boycott, organized by the Protestant Women's Aid, against goods from the Union of South Africa. I didn't want to eat any fruit of apartheid; I really knew quite a lot about it; but somehow I just couldn't bring myself to say to the gentleman in front of me, "Don't buy anything from South Africa; it tastes like blood. You shouldn't help these racists!" I just could not bring myself to make myself ridiculous and stand there alone against the nice saleswoman, the polite older gentleman and the lovely Outspan oranges.

I believe it is normal to be afraid of isolation, just as it is normal to be vulnerable without always going around wearing a crash helmet and gas mask. Of all the photographs which I've seen recently, the ones which have frightened me the most are the ones where the police are running around in crash helmets and gas masks to protect nuclear power plants. The robotlike figures frighten me because they don't have any more contact with the population against whom they are being used: their own bodies are no longer touched; they can't hear what others say; they don't breathe the gas from the chemical weapons. I ask myself how alone the young policemen are behind their packaging. How alone they must be, to produce isolation in others.

The road from the vaccinated peacelessness of "normal" life to consciously and militantly taking a stand for peace frightens people, because it first of all appears to lead into isolation.

"Aren't you talking a little too much about peace?" the school principal recently asked a young untenured colleague—a hidden threat in a paternalistic tone. We have to get through this stage of threat, intimidation, censorship and self-censorship, to find another, new solidarity. If I look for an image which is the opposite of the unrecognizably masked policemen, the two thousand women of the Women's Pentagon Action occur to me, who demonstrated against armaments for the first time in November 1980. They joined hands and surrounded the five-sided building; when they blocked the entrances and were cleared away, other women took their place. Many of them were arrested and sentenced.

The reports of these women, many of them taking part in such an action for the first time, portray exactly this passage from fear, insecurity, self-doubt and unclarity about one's own role to a new self-confidence. "The Pentagon has got to go!" This new self-confidence gives the women who took part a new feeling of self-worth. They are no longer ready to swallow everything, and one can hardly ask whether Reagan's life-threatening politics helped liberate them personally as well.

Occasionally I hear of tensions between consciously-living women and the larger anti-militarist movement. Which is more important, people ask, women's liberation or peace? Should we women sacrifice ourselves—again—in the service of the larger common project? Is there a priority of survival?

I think the question is posed wrongly. Of course survival logically precedes liberation from oppression. But it certainly can't be an either-or question here, or even a matter of one thing coming after the other in time. We want both. Two historical examples:

The women who, at the time of Germany's rearmament, were involved in the Easter March and in the struggle against atomic death had learned during and after the war to stand on their own. They had learned to get along without a husband, father or protector. Under the great pressure of suffering they experienced personal liberation; they were economically self-reliant and also emotionally not entirely dependent. Personal emancipation from the traditional role models, and struggle for the survival of the next generation as well, were a necessity and a unity for them.

During the Vietnam War I came to know some Vietnamese women of a generation which had a much longer way to go from the traditional way of life of an Asian woman to responsible participation in a liberation struggle. Here too, as in other third world countries, personal liberation did not take place outside of, but within the framework of, general national liberation.

What we can learn from these sisters is the unity of what we call liberation. As long as enough poison gases for all of humanity are stockpiled in our country, West Germany, none of us can feel free. Today we must see freedom—certainly not exclusively, but indispensably—as freedom from the capacity for overkill.

In choosing the life of everyone, even those who come after us, I have also chosen myself.

From this point of view, I'd like to ask two practical questions: Is the peace movement ready for women? And is the women's movement ready for peace?

Are the people who work in the peace movement capable of recognizing and combatting the obvious sexism of our culture? It is clear that even a man who is fighting for peace is not, through his anti-militarist convictions, automatically freed from the sexism to which he was trained. For that one needs more consciousness and sensitivity. Even friends of peace must learn to listen to those who normally are not listened to, namely women. Where then could we bring our demands, for example, to be visible as women, if not in the movement for more peace and more democracy? It is unjust and premature, if we become resigned in relation to "the" men, as though they could never learn peace! We must take a couple of pedagogical responsibilities seriously, precisely in the peace movement, and teach the men, instead of despairing of them!

The other question: Are women ready for peace? In the American feminist movement I sometimes worry that the women's alternative culture bypasses such central questions as armaments, and reduces itself, so to speak, to a middle class movement. Now, too, in the reawakening of the peace movement in the United States, individual groups like the Women's Pentagon Action are involved in struggling against the new escalation of madness, but others are still exclusively concerned with the struggles for emancipation of the "professional-managerial class." But it is clear to more and more women how large political decisions control precisely the fate of the multiply oppressed; we ought to get used to thinking of older black unemployed women, when we read how many billions Reagan wants to throw into chemical warfare.

We have to responsibly ask others, but also ourselves, these questions. Is the peace movement really "peaceful," that is, has it gotten beyond the Cain and Abel game? Does it know that peace needs women?

And is the women's movement a movement of humanity? Does it have a general interest, as its best representatives claim—because in a sexist society which oppresses women, men can't become human beings either. Can the women's movement thus help carry the concern of humanity—peace? Will we be that strong, always becoming stronger?

These questions will only be answered in our lived praxis. The questions belong in the peace movement; they cannot be settled by agreements made ahead of time.

To work for peace means to work for one's own liberation and vice versa. This condition of working, struggling, organizing—in a word, life—Jesus, in the Sermon on the Mount, calls by an old word, "Blessed." "Happy are the peacemakers." Unhappy are those who don't take part. Those who wrote for peace are "blessed" now, not just later. Even when we experience defeat, we come into a condition where we regret nothing more.

We reach a point where we cannot turn back. After that point, all return into private self-development is cut-off. Hollanditis is a contagious disease. "Free the world from nuclear weapons, and start in Holland!" The poster in front of me shows an old lady with little curls and little boots, kicking the bombs away. It expresses indignation, rage and strength. We don't have to explain anything more to this old lady. One of her sisters explained on British television, in response to the question what she thought about the new weapons, "I am a civilized woman.

These weapons are uncivilized. I refuse them." Women who work to free the world from nuclear weapons become free themselves as well. There is no other liberation than that which comes through struggle, tears, prison and perhaps more. If we want peace, then we women must struggle for it: hopefully with and if necessary without the men—but we women, in any case.

Mary Jo Leddy

Exercising Theology in the Canadian Context

With the awareness that theology does not drop from some universal sky, there has been a flowering of various theologies from the soil of human experience. Indeed, the shift from a conceptual to a contextual sense of theology, associated with the period after Vatican II, has resulted in one of the most fertile periods in the thinking of the Church. Yet Canada seems noticeably barren in this respect. Why?

The question is not merely academic. Small groups, north of the 49th parallel, are working for justice with this worry: Can the seeds of justice strike deep in the Canadian church if theology has not done its bit to help till the soil of Canadian experience?

Such a question jogs the mind and then leaves it exhausted. It is a difficult task to ground theology in Canadian experience when most Canadians don't know the ground on which they are standing.

This essay, then, is something in the nature of a series of warm-up exercises in preparation for doing theology in the Canadian context.

We Canadians are beginning to learn to walk on our own ground, to stand in our own place. We are slow to take our own history seriously, to make judgments about it, to make decisions from within it and to take action from our own point of departure. This general inability to reflect on our own experience arises from the fundamental fact that ours is a colonial existence. Indeed, we are so subtly, but so surely, colonialized that we do not often reflect on the fact that we are (and always have been) a colony. We have been a colony of France, then of England, and, now, of the United States.

One of our key characteristics as colonials is that we have learned that the point of reference for our lives is elsewhere. As Northrop Frye, one of the most penetrating interpreters of Canadian culture, has said: "Canadians know that the head office is elsewhere." Canadians know that the important decisions affecting our lives are made in the courts and boardrooms of Paris, London, New York and Washington. Similarly, we have internalized (as fact) that the centers of culture and learning are elsewhere. Our point of reference is always elsewhere—*there* but not *here.*

According to Frye, the most liberating question which a people in a colonial culture can ask is: "Where is here?" A culture which strongly defines itself may have the luxury of asking existential questions such as "Who am I?" Not so in a colonial context. Here the question "Who am I?" cannot be completely answered without asking "Where is here?"

It is not too difficult to see how this colonial mentality has been reinforced by the structures of the Roman Catholic Church. The head office, of course, is in Rome and we all too easily see ourselves as a branch plant Church which simply implements decisions which are made elsewhere. It has become almost second nature to us to try to transplant full-grown theologies and over-ripe Church structures from elsewhere. For a long time, the theologians in our colony have tended to think that the only theology worth its name had to be imported from Europe.

More recently, we are turning to the United States for the "latest" in theology or spirituality. Looking further south, we are beginning to take Latin America as the significant point of reference for models of action and reflection. We don't seem grounded enough to make a judgment as to whether the categories of thought and action, which have grown out of a different experience, really fit the reality of Canada. For example: we take the categories of oppressor/oppressed which have an internal coherence with the extreme social conditions of Latin America and use them in an attempt to do a socio-economic analysis of Canada. Left out of this analysis is the not insignificant fact that

Canada is a predominantly middle-class reality. (A fact which Karl Marx himself, given his sense of the revolutionary importance of the middle class, would never ignore.)

This is not a statement about the historic importance of what is happening *there*—in Latin America. It is a statement about what is not happening *here.* It may be that one of the reasons why justice/liberation efforts in Canada have failed to move beyond small groups of the "already converted" is that the language and approach involved in such efforts seem strange and foreign imports to the average Canadian. One wonders how we can build an authentic bridge in solidarity with liberation efforts elsewhere, a bridge between *here* and *there,* when we don't know where here is. Without a measure of social self-consciousness about their own context, Canadians will engage in solidarity efforts in ways which will further diminish their own identity and/or unconsciously reinforce patterns of domination elsewhere.

Yet it is as hard for justice groups (as it is for most Canadians) to take *here* seriously. We colonials tend to feel the action is anywhere else but here. We have a nagging sense that we don't count for much in any global sense and that perhaps we are, as others say, so boring.

In the past few years, there have been some attempts to develop what has been called "a Canadian liberation theology." However, with a few notable exceptions (Gregory Baum and Douglas Hall), most of these efforts resemble a scissors-and-te theology. Cut out some social facts and paste together with some quotes from Scripture, and voilà—a made-in-Canada theology!

Obviously a socio-economic analysis and some reference to biblical history are constitutive elements of any Canadian theology. However, these elements will not automatically lead to an articulation of a theology which helps to liberate a faith response from within the Canadian context. Such a theology must engage our imaginations, the minds of our hearts. Between the facts of our Canadian society and theological reflection on them, we need the mediating images of poets and artists, the revealing stories of writers, to give us some decisive insight into our reality here.

The artist brings a particular gift to a theology which is still in inchoate form. Artists "name" the reality of a culture—often before they or we "know" it in any conceptual or analytic form. Indeed, in the exercise of art, "naming" coincides with "knowing."

Thus, in search of the words which will help to articulate a theology which is fitting for Canada, I will turn briefly to some of the images in Canadian literature which reveal where here is. Within the limits of this essay, this search will be confined to literature and to English Canadian literature.

One of the striking things, in the best examples of Canadian literature, is the "sense of place." These stories are grounded in some region of the country, and the more grounded or located the story, the more universal its appeal. Regional images of sky and land, trees and rocks, etc., become interpretive symbols of the relationship of human beings to the world in which they live. The images are as diverse as the regions of the country itself. Yet, there is one image which is key to understanding each region and the country as a whole—*snow.*

Since the time of the first settlers, Canadians have struggled to survive in the white cold of winter. This was the most obvious and dramatic aspect of a wider struggle with the daunting forces of nature.

There is a significant difference between the Canadian and American experience of nature. The early Americans felt themselves stretched and made bigger by the vastness of their country. The space created an invitation to dominate and explore. In American literature, there is a dominant image of the frontier where violence becomes a way of life, where lone rangers walk tall.

However, Canadians felt dwarfed and threatened by the vast spaces of land. The white north did not yield as easily to domination as did the wild west. The Canadian response to the nature of the land was the desire to survive. And survival as a sociopolitical pattern would take quite a different shape from the patterns of domination which shaped American society.

Even today, Canadians are fascinated by stories of those who survive airplane crashes in the north. The struggle to survive the forces of nature has now become more symbolic than real—symbolic of the country's efforts to survive as one political reality, symbolic of humanity's efforts to survive the global ecological crises.

Canadians developed certain social habits of being in the course of their struggle with the forces of nature: frugality, caution, discipline and endurance. They also developed what Northrope Frye has called a "garrison mentality." Against the vast unconsciousness of nature, Canadians erected their little outposts of civilization. Physical and psychological barriers were constructed to protect small and isolated communities. Within these garrisons, there developed an overwhelming need of and respect for law and order. These beleaguered communities were bound together by law, and the greatest social vices became those of disobedience, individualism, audacity and quitting.

In its worst form, the garrison mentality generated an unquestioning acceptance of authority and a stifling sense of conformism. In its best form, the life of the garrison helped Canadians develop a social experience of community based on cooperation and consensus.

The contemporary Canadian struggle to survive is no longer focused on the forces of nature. With snow blowers and skidoos, we have become more at ease in our land. Technology has enabled us to tame many of the demons of nature which we used to struggle against. Thus, while we continue to be fascinated by the wilderness we are no longer fearful of it. Nature is now our playground, our place of escape from the uncontrollable forces which seem to threaten our cities—not from without but from within. Canadians today seem more threatened by vast socioeconomic forces over which we have no control. Survival has become a social struggle.

In this contemporary situation, it would be important for a Canadian theology to attempt to articulate the liberating and/or enslaving dimensions of the present social patterns which have been shaped by the garrison experience. A Canadian theology, for example, would have to be grounded in a fundamental sense of community. Yet, such a theology would have to develop a view of the person-in-community which moves beyond the cultural bias, in Canada, of communal conformism without lapsing into the American cultural bias in favor of individualism.

A Canadian political theology would also need to take account of the inherent conservatism which developed through the garrison experience. The peculiar shape of Canadian conservativism places it in political opposition to liberalism but not against radicalism. Indeed, Canadian conservativism has produced a peculiar political type called the "Red Tory," a type of social critic which can be found in all shapes and sizes on the political left and right in the country.

To "name" the Canadian political experience, one must turn to the story of the origins of Canada, a story which is quite different from that of the founding of America. The pilgrims to America left the old world in search of a new order and they founded a nation through revolution. The drafters of the Constitution listed "life, liberty and the pursuit of happiness" as the supreme values of the new nation.

In the story of the origins of Canada, there is no such definite break with the past. The British North America Act was something in the nature of a contract which ratified the status quo of the time—a status quo which tensely balanced the claims of two peoples, two languages. One of the most formative influences in the early history of Canada was the influx of those British subjects who chose to remain loyal to the Crown at the time of the American revolution. Through successive waves of immigration, the "loyalists" exercised an early and formative influence on the development of the various structures of Canadian society. The "loyalist" resistance to the American way and its critique of the new became characteristic of Canadians in subsequent generations. For those with a "loyalist" mentality Canada becomes a garrison which needs to protect itself from the domination of the American way. Not surprisingly, a garrison nation articulated "law, order and good government" as the basic values of the BNA Act.

All of which has made Canadian history seem rather drab in comparison to the drama of America. Yet, the traditional Canadian suspicion of rampant domination now seems more universally relevant and finds an echo within America itself. Many American Christians are engaged in an intense period of self-examination and even self-doubt. They have begun to see the underside of their own history—a history in which exploration was accompanied by exploitation. They are questioning the myth of progress at any cost which has shaped their nation. They are more suspicious of the technology which they have used to dominate nature and history and which has now come to dominate them.

What some have put down as cautious Canadian conservativism may (in an age of consuming imperialism) become a radical form of political resistance. The Canadian aversion to violence, the effort to build consensus, the suspicion of dominating power and the respect for law have become more relevant in a world in which cooperation has become essential for survival. A Canadian theology would have the central task of articulating the social virtues and the social vices of a stance of survival. Such a theology would have universal import precisely through its grounding in Canadian experience.

However, a Canadian theology must also reflect on the ways in which the experience of this country not only discloses but also distorts the reality of the Gospel.

Now that Canadians are beginning to take their own story more seriously, they are becoming aware that their history is better—and worse—than they had imagined. The underside of Canadian history is being revealed by those who suffered most in the course of that history. The native peoples, who are beginning to tell their own story, are revealing the original political sin upon which Canada has been built. Deprived of their land and dominated by the system of the whites, the native peoples have become a colony within the colony that is Canada.

The Jewish experience of Canada, as articulated by Irving Abella and Harold Troper in their book *None Is Too Many,* has also helped to shatter the myth of Canadian innocence. These two authors have documented the ugly fact that, during the period 1930-45, Canada was more closed to Jewish immigration than any other country in the western world.

The experience of the natives and the Jews is indicative of the experience of many minority groups in Canada. Yet, most Canadians continue to believe in the myth of their collective innocence. It is a characteristic tendency in a colonial country.

Canadians have what could be called "a branch plant morality," which is the ethical correlative of their belief that the decisions are made in a head office which is elsewhere. For better or worse, Canadians tend to place moral and political responsibility elsewhere. Thus, Canadians find it difficult to see the immorality of producing parts for nuclear weapons when the assembly and distribution of those weapons is done south of the border. A Canadian theology would have to articulate the form of responsibility which is called for in a colony which is also a developed nation and a middle power in the world.

The "naming" of the Canadian experience begins to reveal the shape of social sin in this culture. It is an important step toward knowing the kind of theology which will liberate action for justice *here* which will be in authentic solidarity with struggles against injustice elsewhere. It is equally important to name the grounds for hope in the Canadian experience as a way of knowing the forms of social grace which could be affirmed through a Canadian theology. Canadian literature and history are full of stories of small groups of people who survive against the odds, who build something good together. There are few solitary heroes in Canadian literature. We can imagine, then, that the exercise of theology in the Canadian context would find its source and sustaining power in small collectivities of hope.

Afterword

The present collection of essays honoring my engagement in the Church has come as a surprise to me. The idea behind it and the initiative come from Sister Mary Jo Leddy, doctor of philosophy, a leading Catholic spokesperson in Canada, and a major superior of her religious community, and from Sister Mary Ann Hinsdale, doctor of theology and professor at John's Provincial Seminary in Plymouth, Michigan. I am grateful to them and to my friends and colleagues whom the editors have invited to write for this book.

Much of my life has been a surprise to me. The important events of my biography have been gifts out of the blue. Just before World War II, as a boy under sixteen, I was able to leave Germany thanks to a children's transport organized by a British refugee organization. Since I come from a Jewish family, though secular in spirit and nominally Protestant, I would have lost my life in Nazi Germany. A year later, in 1940, working on a farm in Great Britain, I was arrested as a German citizen and transported to Canada with other civilian internees. An unsolicited surprise lifted me out of the European war into safety. After two years in the internment camp, I was released in Canada. Thanks to the initiative of a refugee committee, sparked largely by Constance Hayward, an YWCA activist, the Canadian government was willing to release the young refugees from the camps, provided they would not take jobs away from Canadians. What was needed were sponsors to permit these young men to go to university. When Emma Kaufman, a leader in the YWCA who had spent her life as an active church worker in Japan, sponsored my education, I was released from the camp to attend McMaster

University in Hamilton, Ontario. In 1942 when life was a series of senseless suffering for vast numbers of people in Europe, I was allowed to begin my university education in peace. The sense of having been singled out and gifted so generously may well have been connected with my turn to religion and the Catholic Church in particular, a few years later. For when I did begin studying the Christian texts to find some sense in a senseless world, it was above all the Pauline, Augustinian, Thomistic emphasis on the unsolicited divine initiative that impressed and moved me deeply. God was the giver.

At that time I was grateful to God, the incomprehensible mystery, present as the rescuing power in my life on so many levels, on the external one mentioned above and on the internal ones as well. My encounter with religion was a healing experience. It took me decades before the problem of evil began to overwhelm me, before the oppression and suffering of others were constantly before my eyes, before my gratitude for what had happened to me personally appeared problematic. To what extent do we desert the others, the troubled brothers and sisters, when we give thanks for the good things that happen to us personally? Do survivors of catastrophe give thanks for their rescue, or do they lament before God the destruction of the brothers and sisters? Perhaps I was too young to wrestle with this question after the war.

It was only in the 1970's, moved by the Church's witness in the third world and "the preferential option for the poor," that I learned to mourn and sorrow over the destruction of innocent people in this sinful world. I relived the destruction of European Jewry during the war. Is it possible to retain a sense of being graced and protected by God without building a wall of happiness around one's heart, and keeping the suffering of others at a distance? Or, conversely, is it possible to be in solidarity with people oppressed by political and economic powers without losing the spirit of gratitude and confidence? Is it possible to pray to God whom Christians call the Almighty when no heavenly lightning bolts call a stop to genocide, repressive violence and mass starvation? Who knows the answer to such questions! Christians are able to give thanks to God in an evil world because Jesus himself in his public humiliation gave thanks and kept his faith. Today the prayer of gratitude offered by Christians is accompanied by a yearning for justice.

Is it possible to pray to God after Auschwitz? Johann Baptist Metz replied: it is possible to pray after Auschwitz because people prayed in Auschwitz.

Encounters with God do not leave us unchanged. That is why I am glad that Mary Jo Leddy and Mary Ann Hinsdale decided to call this collection *Faith That Transforms*. That divine grace truly transforms has been a particularly Catholic emphasis, defended at the Council of Trent against the Protestant tendency to regard divine grace primarily as God's favor and forgiveness extended to us despite our sins. Protestants believed that God's acceptance acknowledged in faith produced a new consciousness in Christians out of which they were able to enter into newness of life. In their own way, Protestants also acknowledged the human being in Jesus Christ. Yet at that time, quite inevitably, Catholics and Protestants applied the gracious power of God to transform human life only to individual persons and in some sense to the Christian community. Since then, Christians have asked whether the message of God's power to transform human sinfulness has any meaning for culture and society.

In his now classic *Christ and Culture* (1954), Richard Niebuhr offered a systematic analysis of how Christians have understood the relation of Christ to culture. In the book Niebuhr identified himself with the emerging trend in the Churches to look upon Jesus as the transformer of culture and society. The traditional Catholic position held that grace sanctified the believers, and that great holiness lifted them above culture to a higher realm. Christians who made a radical option for Jesus Christ tended to renounce the world. Niebuhr called this type, "Christ above culture." The Reformation approach, taken up in the twentieth century by neo-orthodoxy and defended in the United States especially by Reinhold Niebuhr, Richard's brother, held that the ever-merciful grace of God summoned believers to utter selflessness beyond the possibility of nature and society, and hence for all their trying Christians ever remained in need of divine forgiveness. Niebuhr called this type "Christ and culture in paradox." We must, and yet we cannot. We must apply the message of the Gospel to the world in which we live, and yet the limits of nature and the social reality are such that we will forever fail. Beyond these two dominant types, Niebuhr detected a third one, which he called "Christ the transformer of culture." With roots in Scripture and Christian antiquity, this trend emerged clearly only after the industrial and democratic revolutions of the nineteenth century when people gained a greater sense that they could change the social order and hence were actually responsible for their social world. Niebuhr pointed to the Anglican theologian, Frederic Maurice, as an important witness to this emerging trend. In the conditions of modern society, many Christians came to believe that the biblical message of Jesus as Savior, Rescuer, Healer and Lord, revealed God's gracious power to transform culture and society.

Richard Niebuhr understood the transformation offered by Christ in a mildly reformist manner. Since he designated Christians who repudiated the world as sectarian, classified them under the type "Christ against culture," and judged their theology to be outside the authentic range of the Gospel message, he had little affinity for the apocalyptical passages in Scripture that announce the inversion of the sinful world. "The rich shall be sent away empty, and the poor shall be filled with good things; the powerful shall be pushed from their thrones, and those of low degree shall be elevated." Yet the apocalyptical promises continue to offer strength and consolation to Christians living under conditions of apartheid and other forms of grave oppression. It may, therefore, be more faithful to people's religious experiences in the Church, if we understand the theological type, "Christ the transformer of culture," more widely than Niebuhr did to include both reformist and radical understandings of God's action in history.

Richard Niebuhr had a prophetic role in the Church. A decade after his book was published, the theological mainstream in the Catholic Church and the Protestant Churches moved toward the recognition of Christ as transformer of the human world. In the Catholic Church this happened at Vatican Council II. At the World Council of Churches, founded in 1948 under the aegis of neo-orthodox theology, a significant change also took place in the 1960's. Under the impact of third world churches, the World Council also came to recognize Jesus Christ as the transformer of culture and society.

At this time in history, I am deeply moved by the witness given by the Church against apartheid and other massive social evils, in contrast with the silence of the churches in the 1930's during European fascism and even the 1950's and 1960's when the churches often claimed aloofness from the world and did not recognize their own social identification with the dominant economic and political structures. Now we see Bishop Desmond Tutu almost daily on television. He represents black and white Christians. The Anglican Church that appointed him bishop is largely made up of white Christians. The same is true of Alan Boesak. He holds a leadership position in international church organizations that are largely white. When the television news showed the groups of clergymen who went to see President Botha in protest against apartheid, I recognized Denis Hurley, Catholic archbishop of Durban, who has resisted the regime for a long time and was recently indicted for treason. What has changed in the Christian church that such public witness has become a daily occurrence? And what has changed in the spiritual experience of faith that so many Christians are willing to take up the cross, expose themselves to danger, and make great personal sacrifices? As I am writing this essay (August 30, 1985), the message has reached us that a good friend, Charles Villa-Vicencio, a Methodist minister and professor of religious studies at Capetown University, has been arrested.

But the new stance of the Church is not only found in South Africa. All over the world there are networks of Christian groups and individual Christians for whom Jesus Christ is the transformer of culture and society, for whom faith involves discipleship, for whom God's judgment on sin lies upon the injustices built into their own societies, and for whom divine grace is experienced as compassion and empowerment, the power to see society as it is and to resist its evil structures. It is from these Christians, a radical minority, that a new movement in the Church has gone forth, a movement that has come to influence the ecclesiastical leadership. This is what happened at the Conferences of Medellín (1968) and Puebla (1979) when the Latin American bishops committed themselves to "the preferential option for the poor." The same awakening happened when the U.S. Catholic bishops composed their pastoral letters on peace and economic justice. The same influence was operative when the Canadian bishops produced their social messages. The bishops knew themselves to be supported by a network of Christians for whom the Gospel had radical implications. In one of their messages, the Canadian bishops call them "a significant minority," significant because they call the entire Church to greater fidelity.

I realize, of course, that the Catholic authorities have not yet recognized the women's movement as a social justice cause. I realize, moveover, that the Catholic authorities have not yet applied Catholic social teaching to the organization of the Church itself. The principle of subsidiarity receives little attention. Nor is there much ecclesiastical recognition that Christian believers are not objects but subjects in the Church, that is to say, responsible agents called upon to make their contribution to the building of the whole. At this time, Vatican bureaucrats are exercising ugly, dictatorial, non-collegial power that is damaging to individual theologians and harmful to Christian groups in various parts of the Church. Still, the experience of Christ as transformer of society and the arrival of the faith-and-justice movement have so profoundly affected the public stance taken by the Catholic Church that there is reason to marvel and be astounded.

The public acknowledgement of the preferential option for the poor represents a turning point in the life of the Church that may well turn out to be of world-historical importance. What has taken place is, in my opinion, an irreversible process. Bishops in the Church, including members of the curia, who oppose the new trend do not dare to reject the preferential option; instead they try to soften it either by giving it a spiritual, non-material meaning or by asserting that the present order, if slightly reformed, will allow the wealth produced by society to spread further and eventually trickle down to the poor. Yet, in the important ecclesiastical documents, the preferential option is presented as a radical response of faith to divine revelation and an expression of discipleship with disturbing, society-shaking consequences. The preferential option, first formulated at Puebla, has been endorsed by John Paul II in several speeches given in Latin America and in his own, original wording in *Laborem exercens* (1981) as "solidarity of workers and with workers" for the developed countries, and as solidarity of the poor and with the poor for the underdeveloped world. The Canadian bishops have made the preferential option a basic principle of their social teaching, and the U.S. bishops have also endorsed the preferential option, even in a slightly modified sense, in their pastoral on economic justice.

Allow me to clarify what precisely the preferential option for the poor means. The option is grounded in Scripture. After presenting a detailed analysis of the biblical teaching on the poor and God's call for justice, the U.S. pastoral on economic justice concludes that "the option for the poor is a valid interpretation of the biblical witness." This option has taken on different forms. In the Old Testament we read of God's own liberating option for the enslaved people of Israel. This option was later written into the law of Israel, designed to protect the poor and weak from exploitation by the powerful. The prophets opted for the poor when they indicted the kings and the dominant classes for oppression and exploitation. God stood with the poor. To know God meant to do justice. The apocalyptical sections of the Bible revealed the hope that God would vindicate the poor in God's hour of triumph and establish them in a society of justice and peace. In the New Testament, the poor are blessed because their lot will be changed. God's reign is approaching. In the meantime, people are called to have compassion for the poor and be generous in almsgiving. Helping the poor is the public sign of true religion in the biblical traditions, Jewish and Christian. This "compassionate" option for the poor was soon accompanied by what may be called an "ascetical" option. Christians believed that opting for the simple life, following the example of Jesus, they prepared themselves for a deeper relationship with God. They did not idealize destitution, but they believed that a life based on a minimum of material satisfaction was an evangelical vocation. This option has been kept alive in the Church, especially in religious orders. It is being renewed today by many young men and women in the Church who do not have the protection of an order.

For St. Augustine, the option for the poor expressed itself in the refusal to accept the theology of history, proposed by certain bishops, which legitimated the Roman Empire as a special manifestation of God's providence. History, Augustine argued against this imperial theology, was meaningless. What was meaningful was the relentless struggle between self-love and the love of God-and-neighbor going on in society. For St. Thomas the option for the poor meant resistance to the feudal order and support for the townspeople who sought to create a more participatory society. The mendicant orders embodied this rising democratic feeling in their constitutions.

More recently we hear of a "missionary" option for the poor. In parts of Europe where the Church has lost the loyalty of the working class, many priests decided to strengthen their Christian witness by living in the same material circumstances as the workers. The missionary role of poverty was debated in connection with the "Mission de France" after World War II. At the Vatican Council, this option was held up as an ideal for the entire Church. Bishops exchanged their golden rings for rings of brass to symbolize their identification with the ordinary people to whom they address the Christian message. In recent Church documents, we also find references to the "pastoral" option for the poor. This refers to the decision of religious organizations, such as dioceses and religious orders, to plan their use of resources, including personnel, first of all in the service of the poor. The pastoral option also affects the direction of Catholic schools, colleges, hospitals, parishes and other institutions.

Finally, the Puebla Conference gave the definition of the "preferential" option for the poor, which determined the Church's relationship to the social world of which it was part (nn. 1134–1152). Needless to say, the preceding options for the poor retain their validity. Today, however, they must all be complemented by a conscious faith commitment to social justice. Puebla defined the preferential option of the poor as a double commitment of Christians: (a) to look at the social reality from the perspective of the poor (the hermeneutic dimension); (b) to give public witness to solidarity with these poor (the activist dimension).

This is a radical principle. Allow me to clarify the preferential option with a few remarks. It is not, as some critics have suggested, equivalent to the Marxist option for the proletariat. In the original Marxism the industrial working class was regarded as the bearer of revolution, and hence the struggle of and with the proletariat was the historical instrument for initiating a society beyond domination. The Church's preferential option for the poor is a much wider call for solidarity among and with all the people at the bottom and in the margin of society. At the bottom this includes the workers, industrial and clerical, employed and unemployed, urban and rural, and the poor in general; and in the margin, a category that cuts across the preceding one, this includes the people pushed to the edge, the native peoples, certain ethnic groups, the handicapped, the neglected aged, and to a large extent women. In countries that suppress the worship of God, this includes the believers deprived of their freedom. The option of the poor expresses solidarity with all the people on whose shoulders the existing society has placed unjust and crushing burdens.

We note, moreover, that the preferential option is a transcendental principle. For in new historical circumstances, after a revolution or other significant reconstructions of society, another group or sector may find itself marginalized, and then the preferential option demands solidarity with these new victims. While the temptation of people suffering oppression is to envy the oppressor and desire to replace him and thus to become. the oppressor themselves, the preferential option for the poor gives rise to a different imagination, the yearning for a qualitatively different society, a society closed to God's "shalom." Some critics have objected that the preferential option expresses a patronizing spirit because it seems to appeal only to Christians who are not poor themselves. Yet Latin American liberation theology has shown that the masses of the marginalized people are in need of a conscious option for themselves: this option, summoned forth by their encounter with Christ and the Christian community, delivers them from the passivity, fatalism and powerlessness in which they have been imprisoned. The preferential option speaks also to the poor. In Latin America, the class distance is so enormous that the people who live in constant insecurity readily refer to themselves as the poor. In North America, the dream of upward mobility, though increasingly unrealistic, makes the people at the base of society unwilling to think of themselves as "the poor." People feel that this is not a respectable word. For this reason, I usually refer to the victims of society as people at the bottom and in the margin.

The preferential option undoubtedly implies an overcoming of the organic view of society that was part of traditional Catholic social teaching. Here society was looked upon as a closely-knit community, a many-leveled body politic, with people on each level serving the common good. The well-being of this society depended on the fidelity of all people to the duties and virtues appropriate to their social rank. Social reform in this organic view demanded the conversion to greater justice on all levels of society. The preferential option, first formulated in Latin American society, implied a conflictual view of society, not so much in the Marxian sense where a single system of domination, the economic one, divided the population into masters and servants, but more in a Weberian sense where society was perceived as a complex structure of domination that imposed its will on the people. The Weberian perception of society as a conflictual process involving the dominant structures and the countervailing trends promoted by the disadvantaged has a certain affinity with the more recent Catholic social teaching. The Canadian bishops have gone further than anyone in elaborating this new, more conflictual Catholic social theory.

The preferential option for the poor is a radical principle. It defines the meaning of discipleship in today's world. It entails spiritual, intellectual, cultural and political involvement. In the ecclesiastical sciences, the preferential option calls for the study of the biblical texts from the perspective of the victims of society; it initiates a new approach to the study of Church history; it generates a systematic theology that brings out the transformative power of divine revelation; it calls for an ethics that pays primary attention to the liberation of people from oppression; and it creates a spirituality and forms of contemplation that recognize God's partiality for the poor and God's promises to deliver them from oppression. Some Christian teachers and scholars have engaged in this revisionist enterprise for many years.

The preferential option also demands that we look upon our own society and its relationship to the global system from the perspective of the victims. This brings Christians into dialogue with the social sciences. There are sociologists who question the value-neutral, objective approach that predominates in most university departments. They argue persuasively that every glance at society, even with the tools of social science, comes from a particular perspective. Unless we are critically aware, we tend to look upon society from the viewpoint of our friends, our associates, our own class. More than that, these sociologists argue that sociological research and theory help to steer the public perception of society and hence exercise a considerable political influence. Only if social scientists do their research and thinking from an emancipatory commitment will they discover the damaging features in the social order and help to overcome them in practice. The sociologists' emancipatory commitment has a close affinity with the Christian preferential option.

The preferential option sheds a critical light on the culture in which we live. Culture is constituted by the values, symbols, customs, laws and institutions that mediate an ethos among a people and project a guiding vision for their society. The preferential option inevitably discloses the ambiguity of culture, brings out its political content, reveals the extent to which culture protects the dominant structures and uncovers the more hidden symbols in the culture that nourish the dream of an alternative, more humane society. The preferential option here becomes a key for the interpretation of literature and the arts.

The preferential option has practical political significance because it includes not only a new hermeneutics of the social reality but also demands public action in solidarity with society's victims. To engage in such action Christians are in need of a social analysis of injustice and oppression in their midst. But since theologians are not usually trained in sociology, how can they involve themselves in a critical analysis of this kind? How can

Catholics in the parishes take part in such critical reflections? To respond to these needs an extraordinary development has taken place in the Catholic Church: the bishops themselves have produced and sponsored pastoral letters that name the social evils in society, analyze the structures of oppression, and provide conceptual tools that enable Christians to engage in critical examination of what goes on in their neighborhood, in their country and in the global society. The new Catholic social teaching is presented in the pastoral documents of the Latin American and North American bishops, supported by the social theory of John Paul II's *Laborem exercens.*

In my opinion, the North American bishops have taken the preferential option for the poor more seriously than most Catholic institutions, parishes, schools, colleges and hospitals. The bishops, in my opinion, are ahead of Catholic theological faculties. While most Catholic theologians have come to emphasize love, justice and peace as God's redemptive gifts to humanity, they tend to remain rather vague about what this message means in North American society. Calls for justice in general do not make enemies. If recommendations of peace are broad enough, they could even be used by speech writers for the government. Yet the American and Canadian bishops have made enemies. In their peace pastoral, the American bishops ask Catholics to influence public opinion so that all Americans, including the bishops, will sorrow over the dropping of the atomic bomb in 1945; only such mourning, the bishops believe, will create the public consciousness required for avoiding a nuclear solution for present political problems. I marvel at the bishops' courage. In the 1983 statement on the economic crisis, the Canadian bishops analyzed the crisis of capitalism and in particular the transformation of capital in Canada. Unless capital and technology are harnessed by society to serve basic human needs, the bishops say, they become an enemy rather than an ally of human development. This sentence made the bishops many enemies. I regret, of course, that the Catholic bishops, probably under orders from Rome, hesitate to recognize the oppressive structures of patriarchy. Still, in their effort to translate the preferential option for the poor into the North American context, they have set a good example. They have inspired many.

Over the last decade or so, there has emerged in the Church a strong faith-and-justice movement, made up of groups and individuals, lay and clerical, who had new religious experiences, who understood divine revelation as a transformative message, and in whose hearts love gave birth to a passionate yearning for justice. This movement began in Latin America and other third world countries; it was seconded by black theology, Mexican American collective aspirations, and the struggles of other Christian groups exploited in North American society; it was strengthened by Christian women who believed that the divine promises given in Christ included their liberation from patriarchal subjugation, and defended and enhanced by liberation theology and political theology of North America and Europe; and it was blessed and supported by many episcopal documents and occasionally even papal encyclicals. This movement exists in all the churches. For Christians moved by the preferential option, ecumenical cooperation and communion are spontaneous. These Christians reach out for allies among other non-Christian religious communities and among secular groups. When these Christians meet Jews who cherish the ancient prophetic tradition, they feel bound to them in the same faith. One must recognize, of course, that the faith-and-justice Christians in the Church are not fully agreed on their analysis of social evil nor on the strategies of their social involvement. The differences are here considerable. Still, they have a strong sense that they belong together, that they live out of the same Gospel, that they are brothers and sisters who must support one another. While in secular society reformists and radicals easily become enemies, it is my impression that in the North American church reformists and radicals remain friends. Robert Drinan and Daniel Berrigan defend one another. It is a remarkable phenomenon that faith-and-justice Catholics admire the radical evangelical community with its publication, *Sojourners,* and know themselves to be alive by the same spirit, even if they disagree with some of the positions taken by the review. (*The Ecumenist,* edited by me and published by Paulist Press, promotes the unity of Christians in the Church's social ministry and as such sees itself as serving this faith-and-justice movement.)

What is the sociology of this movement in the North Amer-

ican Church? The movement is built around identifiable Christian "groups" and "centers," it communicates with the wider
Catholic and Christian community through newsletters, pamphlets, journals and books, and it is supported to a considerable
extent by funds made available by diocesan organizations, religious orders and Catholic educational institutions. The Christian
"groups" are of two kinds: there are action groups made up of
Christians struggling against the subjugation inflicted on them
(native peoples, blacks, Mexican Americans, Puerto Ricans, refugees, immigrants, unemployed workers, women), and there are
solidarity groups of Christians who, though more privileged, support these struggles by action, prayer and influence on public
opinion (committees to support the right of native peoples; to
demand justice for refugees, immigrants, the unemployed, and
people of color; to defend human rights in Latin America and the
Philippines; to support the revolution in Nicaragua and the struggle against apartheid in South Africa; and to promote more generous support for the aged, the handicapped and retarded). And
then there are Christian "centers": they are institutes of various
size, some very small, that promote the faith-and-justice movement through prayer and worship, social science research, theological reflection, religious education, publishing newspapers,
pastoral ministry, strategy studies, and other forms of activity.
These centers are usually attached to religious orders, diocesan
organizations, Catholic colleges or other church agencies. While
the "groups" mentioned above tend to look after their own
financing, the "centers" tend to be financed through the church
institutions to which they are attached. The support given by religious orders, especially of women's communities, deserves special mention. The groups often produce newsletters, and the centers produce publications of various kinds, from pamphlets to
books.

Part of the sociology of the movement are individul Christians for whom the Gospel is a transformist message. They stand
with the more clearly defined groups and centers, they join the
prayer services, they read the literature, they offer solidarity, they
involve themselves in action. Among them are theologians who
understand their work as a service to liberation. The important

names that come to mind are Rosemary Ruether, Robert McAfee Brown and Matthew Lamb in the United States, and Johann Baptist Metz and Dorothee Sölle in Germany. There are many others who deserve to be mentioned. Among these Christians are journalists and religious educators who communicate the trans-formist meaning of the Gospel, community organizers, teachers, social workers, mystics, political leaders, social activists, men and women of all ranks who support the faith-and-justice move-ment and are spiritually nourished by it. Last but not least, the sociology of the movement includes the blessing extended by the Catholic bishops, especially by the bishops' conferences of the United States and Canada and by particular bishops whose hearts have been touched by the preferential option. While the partici-pants in the movement often moan and groan about the hierar-chy, and regret Rome's refusal to recognize the aspiration of women as a social justice cause, Catholics realize very well that the vitality of the movement in their Church is due to a consid-erable extent to the fact that the preferential option for the poor has been endorsed by the Church's magisterium.

May I add that the contours of the movement are by no means hidden. Catholics belonging to a given locality are able to name the action and solidarity groups as well as the social justice centers in their region, they know the priests and religious men and women who support the movement, they are acquainted with the Christians in schools, colleges, unions, city organizations and other public institutions for whom social justice is a priority, they know the churches or chapels where prayer services are held for peace, justice and human rights. These are the assemblies that commemorate the martyrdom of Archbishop Oscar Romero. And if they look for signatures, for helpers, and for people ready to be counted in demonstrations, they know whom to ask and whom not to ask. What is typical in North America is that in any given locality, this movement defines itself ecumenically.

What faith and justice mean in Canada, in English-speaking Canada and Quebec, is an issue that engages many Christians, among them Douglas Hall and Mary Jo Leddy. We learn from the social messages composed by our church leaders, Catholic, Anglican, and Protestant; we are in dialogue with Canadian political thought and political economy; and we participate in various ways in struggles and actions for justice in Canadian society.

How do the majority of Catholics in the parishes look upon this movement in the Church? Some of them, especially among the affluent and powerful, are angry; they are particularly angry with the bishops and certain papal pronouncements that bless the preferential option for the poor. It is my impression, however, that the great majority of Catholics who have not been personally touched by this movement look upon it with admiration and puzzlement, as they may look upon religious life in the Church. They may not feel called to it, but they are open to new experiences of life and solidarity, and if the Spirit so touches them, they are quite willing to rethink their place and mission in life.

In my work as critical theologian, as teacher, as intellectual, I have a strong sense that I belong to a movement in the Church. I do not think alone, in isolation from others; my thinking, teaching and writing are generated by an ongoing conversation with others. What I try to express is not simply my own reflection, nor simply an account of my own Christian experience; I want to interpret and clarify the Christian experiences emerging in the faith-and-justice movement, in reliance on Scripture and the Catholic tradition, and in dialogue with social and political science. I am helped to do this by many theologians, religious educators and social critics who understand themselves as part of the movement. The solidarity I share with Jews committed to prophecy and secular friends marked by an emancipatory commitment offers me personal support and helps me in my theological work. It cannot be denied that the preferential option produces sadness and mourning. It demands that we keep looking at the great suffering in the world inflicted by the few on the many, apartheid in South Africa, world hunger, U.S. sponsored terrorism against Nicaragua, Soviet repression in Eastern Europe—an endless litany. We escape despair only if we have profound experiences of brotherhood (sisterhood) with the crucified and risen Christ, with the saints including Oscar Romero, with Christian brothers and sisters in the movement, and with the allies of the heart in Judaism and secular society. Because of the divine promises made in the Scriptures we remain hopeful. Because of God's presence to the poor, to those who mourn, to the peacemakers, to those who hunger and thirst for justice, we are often even capable of remaining cheerful.

This takes me back to the beginning of this essay. The transformative understanding the the Gospel and the faith-and-justice movement generated by it is in keeping with the classical theology of grace with emphasis on the divine initiative. The preferential option does not nourish a Promethean dream; it is not of Pelagian inspiration; it is not even, if I may be forgiven, Molinist. The struggle of people to assume responsibility for their world and create a just society is ultimately due to God's gracious presence to them. There is a passive dimension in human action. Before they engage in social struggles, people are touched, stirred, made restless, and overwhelmed by longings for justice. Before they struggle, people are freed from distorted vision and made to see clearly. As people engage themselves in solidary action, they are lifted out of their small circle and experience an explosion of the heart. Action is always carried by *passio,* by a passive dimension, by receiving transcendent gifts. People are called to be subjects of their history because God has created them as subjects and because God's redemptive presence to them empowers them to overcome the obstacles that prevent them from being the responsible agents of their world. At the same time, subject of history in its totality, as Johann Baptist Metz has so well said, is only the One who has power over the dead: because of this God, our solidarity with victims and all who struggle for justice extends not only in the present but also reaches into the past.

Stephen J. Schäfer, compiler

Chronological Bibliography of the Works of Gregory G. Baum

The following bibliography of the works of Professor Gregory G. Baum is divided into two main sections. The first section, entitled "Books," contains those volumes authored and edited by Professor Baum. The difference is indicated in the listing. The second section, entitled "Articles," contains articles, contributions to symposia, chapters in books, introductions, prefaces, editorials, newspaper articles and book reviews. Both sections are arranged chronologically with the items alphabetized within each year. Reprints, revised editions, and translations are listed immediately following the original appearance of the item. One exception to this is material found in *Concilium,* the multi-volume, international review of theology which is published simultaneously in seven languages (English, French, German, Dutch, Spanish, Portuguese, and Italian). Articles and editions here are listed according to the English edition only, with the exception of two volumes which failed to have an English edition published. The latter two volumes are cited according to the French edition (see "Books," 1975 and 1976).

Throughout the goal has been to compile a complete listing of Professor Baum's work to date, including writings on both scholarly and popular levels. To the best of our knowledge the list is complete with two known exceptions: shorter book reviews and newspaper articles have been included but no thorough attempt has been made to be exhaustive in our search here. No doubt there are other exceptions to the completeness of this list, for which the compiler accepts responsibility for their omission.

BOOKS

1958

That They May Be One: A Study of Papal Doctrine (Leo XIII— Pius XII). London: Bloomsbury Publishing Co. Ltd., 1958. (American edition: Westminster, Maryland: The Newman Press.) French edition: *L'unité chrétienne d'après la doctrine des papes de Léon XIII à Pie XII.* Traduit de l'anglais par André Renard. Paris: Éditions du Cerf, 1961 (*Unam Sanctum*, No. 35).

1961

The Jews and the Gospel: A Re-Examination of the New Testament. London: Bloomsbury Publishing Co. Ltd., 1961. (American edition: Westminster, Maryland: The Newman Press.) Revised second edition with new title and preface: *Is The New Testament Anti-Semitic? A Re-Examination of the New Testament.* Glen Rock, N.J.: Paulist Press, Deus Books, 1965. German edition: *Die Juden und das Evangelium. Eine Überprüfung des Neuen Testaments.* Aus dem Englischen übersetzt von Elisabeth Strakosch. Einsiedeln: Benziger Verlag, 1963. French edition: *Les Juifs et L'Évangile.* Traduit de l'anglais par J. Mignon. Paris: Éditions du Cerf, 1965 (*Lectio Divina*, No. 41). Spanish edition: *Los Judios y el Evangelio.* Traduccion del ingles e introduccion del Rvdo. P. Jesus Alverez del Carmen. Madrid: Aguilar, 1965.

1962

Progress and Perspectives: The Catholic Quest for Christian Unity. New York: Sheed and Ward, 1962. (British edition with the title: *The Quest for Christian Unity.* London: Sheed & Ward, Stag Books, 1963.) Paperback edition with the title: *The Catholic Quest for Christian Unity.* Glen Rock, N.J.: Paulist Press, Deus Books, 1965. Dutch edition: *Kerk en Eenheid.* Uit het engels vertaald door Josef Mertens, pr. Roermond-Maaseik: J. J. Romen & Zonen Uitgevers, 1964.

1964

Editor of *Ecumenical Theology Today*. Glen Rock, N.J.: Paulist Press, Deus Books, 1964.

1967

Editor of *Ecumenical Theology No. 2*. Glen Rock, N.J.: Paulist Press, Deus Books, 1967.

Editor of *The Future of Belief Debate*. New York: Herder and Herder, 1967.

1968

The Credibility of the Church Today. New York: Herder & Herder, 1968. German edition: *Glaubwürdigkeit. Zum Selbstverständnis der Kirche*. Deutsche übersetzung von Johannes Fischer und Franz Schmalz. Freiburg: Herder, 1969.

1969

Faith and Doctrine: A Contemporary View. New York: The Newman Press, 1969. [The David S. Schaff Lectures, Pittsburgh Theological Seminary, 1968.] (Paperback edition: New York: Paulist Press, 1969.) German edition: *Plädoyer für den Glauben. Ein Buch für Suchende und Zweifler*. Aus dem Englischen übersetzt von Herta-Maria und Josef Fink. Graz: Styria, 1971.

1970

Man Becoming: God in Secular Experience. New York: The Seabury Press, 1970. (Paperback edition in *The Seabury Library of Contemporary Theology*, New York: The Seabury Press, 1979.) Spanish edition: *El Hombre como Possibilidad: Dios in La Experiencia Secular*. Lo tradujo al castellano: Pedro R. Santidrian. Madrid: Ediciones Cristiandad, 1974.

1972

New Horizon: Theological Essays. New York: Paulist Press, 1972.

1973

Editor with Andrew Greeley of *The Persistence of Religion. Concilium,* vol. 81. New York: Herder and Herder, 1973.

1974

Editor with Andrew Greeley of *The Church as Institution. Concilium,* vol. 91. New York: Herder and Herder, 1974.

1975

Editor with Andrew Greeley of *Les Intellectuels dans L'Église. Concilium,* 101. Paris: Editions Beauchesne, 1975. (NB: No English edition.)

Editor of *Journeys: The Impact of Personal Experience on Religious Thought.* New York: Paulist Press, 1975.

Religion and Alienation: A Theological Reading of Sociology. New York: Paulist Press, 1975.

1976

Christian Theology After Auschwitz. London: British Council of Christians and Jews, 1976. (Robert W. Cohen Memorial Lecture.)

Editor with Andrew Greeley of *Les Femmes dans L'Église. Concilium, 111.* Paris: Éditions Beauchesne, 1976. (NB: No English edition.)

1977

Editor with Andrew Greeley of *Ethnicity. Concilium,* vol. 101. New York: The Seabury Press, 1977.

Truth Beyond Relativity: Karl Mannheim's Sociology of Knowledge. Marquette, Wisconsin: Marquette University Press, 1977. (Pere Marquette Theology Lecture.)

1978

Editor with Andrew Greeley of *Communication in the Church. Concilium,* vol. 111. New York: The Seabury Press, 1978.

1979

The Social Imperative: Essays on the Critical Issues That Confront the Christian Churches. New York: Paulist Press, 1979.

1980

Catholics and Canadian Socialism: Political Thought in the Thirties and Forties. Toronto: James Lorimer & Company, Publishers, 1980. (American edition: New York: Paulist Press.)

Editor of *Sociology and Human Destiny: Essays on Sociology, Religion and Society.* New York: The Seabury Press, Crossroad Books, 1980.

Editor of *Work and Religion. Concilium,* vol. 131. New York: The Seabury Press, 1980.

1981

Editor of *Neo-Conservatism: Social and Religious Phenomenon. Concilium,* vol. 141. New York: The Seabury Press, 1981.

1982

Editor with John Coleman of *Church and Racism. Concilium,* vol. 151. New York: The Seabury Press, 1982.

The Priority of Labor: A Commentary on Laborem exercens, *Encyclical Letter of Pope John Paul II.* New York: Paulist Press, 1982.

1983

Editor with John Coleman of *New Religious Movements. Concilium,* vol. 161. New York: The Seabury Press, 1983.

1984

Co-author with Duncan Cameron. *Ethics and Economics: Canada's Catholic Bishops on the Economic Crisis.* Toronto: James Lorimer & Company, 1984.

Editor with John Coleman of *The Sexual Revolution. Concilium,* vol. 173. Edinburgh: T. & T. Clark, 1984.

1985

Editor with John Coleman of *Youth Without a Future? Concilium,* vol. 181. Edinburgh: T. & T. Clark, 1985.

ARTICLES

1959

"Ecumenical Attitudes." *Apostolic Perspectives* 4 (January 1959) 4–8.

1960

"Changes in Protestantism." *Commonweal* 72 (1960) 203–205.

"The World Council of Churches." *Commonweal* 72 (1960) 319–321.

1961

"Approaches to Scripture." *Commonweal* 74 (1961) 71–73.

"Bishops, the Laity and the Second Vatican Council." *Catholic Messenger* 79 (17 August 1961) 5–6.

"The Catholic Position on Natural Law." *The Student World* 54 (1961) 394–398.

"A Catholic-Protestant Confrontation." Review of *Christianity Divided* edited by Heiko A. Oberman and Daniel J. O'Hanlon. New York: Sheed & Ward, 1961; in *Commonweal* 75 (1961) 212–213.

"Catholics, Protestants and the Ecumenical Movement." Review of *The Churches and the Church* by Bernard Leeming. Westminster, Maryland: The Newman Press, 1960, in *Commonweal* 73 (1961) 614–615.

"The Church and the World." *Crosslight* 3 (1961). 14–23.

"Ecumenism: Year-End Roundup." *Ave Maria* 94 (30 December 1961) 18–19.

"Die oekumenische Situation in Amerika." *Augustinianum* 1 (1961) 146–148.

"Promoting Christian Unity." *Guide* 158 (December 1961) 10–12.

"Protestants and Natural Law." *Commonweal* 73 (1961) 427–430. [Reprinted in *Catholic Mind* 59 (1961) 222–229]

"Roman Catholic Theology in Germany Today." *Canadian Journal of Theology* 7 (1961) 258–270.

1962

"Apologetic and Ecumenism Compared." *Catholic World* 196 (October 1962) 14–19.

Review of *Catholic Theology in Dialogue* by Gustave Weigel. New York: Harper, 1961, in *Theological Studies* 23 (1962) 303–305.

"Conflicts and the Council." *Commonweal* 76 (1962) 511–14.

"Dialogue oecuménique ou conversion?" *Maintenant* 1 (1962) 323–324.

"A Difference of Opinion." *Pax Romana Journal* 6 (1962) 3–5, 12.

"An Ecumenical Decline?" *Catholic Messenger* 80 (12 April 1962) 6. [Reprinted in *Commonweal* 76 (1962) 180–181.]

"Ecumenical Dialogue or Conversion?" *Clergy Review* 47 (1962) 585–588.

"End of the Beginning." *Commonweal* 7 (1962) 227–230.

"The Laity and the Council." *Blackfriars* 43 (1962) 59–69.

"Mixed Marriages and the Council." *The Ecumenist* 1 (1962) 23–25. [Reprinted in *Ecumenical Theology Today* edited by Gregory Baum (1964).]

"The Nature of Ecumenical Councils." *The Ecumenist* 1 (1962) 4–6.

"A New Journal." *The Ecumenist* 1 (1962) 1.

"Oecuménisme aux Etats-Unis." *Choisir* 29 (1962) 12–14.

"Pope and Bishops," *The Ecumenist* 1 (1962) 21–23. [Reprinted in *Commonweal* 79 (1963) 188–191, and in *Guide* 183 (December 1963) 3–7.]

"Protestants Look at Mary." *Ave Maria* 95 (14 April 1962) 12–14. [Reprinted in *The Furrow* 13 (1962) 455–461, and with new title "Mary and the Protestants" in *Catholic Digest* 27 (January 1963) 10–13.]

"Public Opinion in the Church." *Insight: A Journal of Opinions* Preview Issue (1962) 4–5.

"The Second Vatican Council and the World Council of Churches." *The Ecumenist* 1 (1962) 2–4.

"Turning Point at the Council." *Commonweal* 77 (1962) 334–337.

1963

"The Aims of the Council: An Analysis of the Pope's Opening Speech." *Crosslight* 4 (1963) 54–60.

"Away from Centralization." *Clergy Review* 48 (1963) 275–279. [Reprinted in *Way* 19 (September 1963) 51–54.]

"Can Catholics Learn from Protestants?" *Frontiers* 14 (1963) 20–24.

"The Catholic Church and the W.C.C." *The Ecumenist* 1 (1963) 92–95. [Reprinted in *Ecumenical Theology Today* edited by Gregory Baum (1964).]

"Clarification of Doctrine as a Source of Renewal." *Catholic World* 196 (1963) 215–222.

"The Community of Believers." *Perspectives* 8 (February 1963) 12–14.

"Confrontation in the Council." *Commonweal* 79 (1963) 311–313.

"Corner Has Been Turned on Church Decentralization." *Catholic Messenger* 81 (28 February 1963) 1ff.

"The Council Culminates Evolution in the Church." *Catholic Messenger* 81 (13 June 1963) 8.

"Dialogue or Conversion?" *Pax Romana Journal* 7 (1963) 17–18.

"The Ecumenical Movement and the Jews." *The Ecumenist* 1

(1963) 36–38. [Reprinted in *Ecumenical Theology Today* edited by Gregory Baum (1964).]

"End of the Deadlock." *Commonweal* 79 (1963) 251–253.

"End of the Session." *Commonweal* 79 (1963) 393–396.

"Fresh Look at Marian Passages Spurred in Montreal." *Catholic Messenger* 81 (15 August 1963) 7.

"Foreword" to *Unity: Man's Tomorrow* by Roger Schutz. New York: Herder and Herder, 1963, pp. 4–6 (A translation of *L'unite, Esperance de Vie.* Taizé: Les Presses de Taizé, 1962.)

"Montreal: Faith and Order." *Commonweal* 78 (1963) 505–511.

"New Spirit at the Council." *Commonweal* 79 (1963) 125–129.

"*Pacem in Terris* and Unity." *The Ecumenist* 1 (1963) 73–75. [Reprinted in *Ecumenical Theology Today* edited by Gregory Baum (1964).]

"Papacy and Episcopacy." *The Ecumenist* 1 (1963) 81–82. [Reprinted in *Ecumenical Theology Today* edited by Gregory Baum (1964).]

"Pope and the Council." *Clergy Review* 48 (1963) 1–11.

"Primacy and Episcopacy: A Doctrinal Reflection." *The Thomist* 27 (1963) 211–221. [Also printed in *Vatican II: The Theological Dimension* edited by Anthony D. Lee. New York: The Thomist Press, 1963, pp. 211–221; reprinted in *Dominicana* 49 (1964) 7–15; and in *Ecumenical Theology Today* edited by Gregory Baum (1964).]

"The Role of Bishops in Relation to the Papacy." *Catholic World* 198 (1963) 94–99.

Review of *That the World May Believe* by Hans Küng. New York: Sheed & Ward, 1963, in *Commonweal* 78 (1963) 404–405.

"Theological Reflections on the Second Vatican Council." *Catholic Messenger* 81 (25 April 1963) 5.

"Triumph for Renewal." *Commonweal* 77 (1963) 434–436.

"What Are Other Churches?" *The Ecumenist* 2 (1963) 1–4.

[Reprinted in *Ecumenical Theology Today* edited by Gregory Baum (1964).]

"What Can the Ecumenical Council Do in Regard to the Jewish People?" *Catholic Messenger* 81 (24 January 1963) 5.

"What You Can Do for Christian Reunion." *Sign* 43 (November 1963) 20–23. (Interview by D. Roche.)

"Who Belongs to the Church?" *The Ecumenist* 1 (1963) 49–51. [Reprinted in *The Living Church* 146 (1963) 8–9; and in *Ecumenical Theology Today* edited by Gregory Baum (1964).]

"Word and Sacrament in the Church." *Thought* 38 (1963) 190–200. [Reprinted as "Introduction" to *Gospel Initiations* by Mother M. Chabanel. Glen Rock, N.J.: Paulist Press, 1963, pp. 9–18; and in *Guide* 187 (April 1964) 3–9.]

1964

"Aspects of Ecumenism." *Focus* 1 (1964) 5–16.

"Books of Conflict." Reviews of *Observer in Rome* by Robert McAfee Brown. Garden City, N.Y.: Doubleday, 1964; *The Open Church* by Michael Novak. New York: Macmillan, 1964; *The Second Session* by Xavier Rynne. New York: Farrar, Straus, 1964; and *The Pilgrim* by Michael Serafian. New York: Farrar, Straus, 1964, in *Sign* 44 (September 1964) 26–27ff.

"Birth Control and the Council." *Commonweal* 81 (1964) 280, 282, 284, 285–286.

"The Blossoming of Vatican II." *Commonweal* 81 (1964) 130–132.

"Can the Church Change Her Position on Birth Control?" in *Contraception and Holiness: The Catholic Predicament* edited by Thomas D. Roberts. New York: Herder & Herder, 1964, pp. 311–344. Italian edition: "La Chiesa può mutare la propria posizione sul controllo delle nascite?" in *Controllo Delle Nascite E Santità Della Famiglia*. Presentati da Thomas D. Roberts. Milano: Rizzoli Editore, 1965, pp. 277–307.

"A Catholic Interpretation of History." in *Ecumenical Theology Today* edited by Gregory Baum. Glen Rock, N.J.: Paulist Press, Deus Books, 1964, pp. 105–118.

"Christians and Jews." *Catholic Digest* 29 (December 1964) 58–60.

"Commentary on *Ecclesiam Suam:* Encyclical Letter of His Holiness Pope Paul VI." in *The Paths of The Church.* Glen Rock, N.J.: Paulist Press, 1964, pp. 3–13.

"Communicatio in Sacris." *The Ecumenist* 2 (1964) 60–62. [Reprinted in *Ecumenical Theology Today* edited by Gregory Baum (1964).]

"The Council, the Press, and Ecumenism." *Catholic Journalist* 15 (July 1964) 7–8ff.

"Drawing Closer Together." in *Steps to Christian Unity* edited by John A. O'Brien. Garden City, N.Y.: Doubleday, 1964, pp. 268–283. [Reprinted in *Ave Maria* 100 (5 September 1964) 14–15f. (12 September 1964) 10–11.]

"*Ecclesiam Suam* and Christian Unity." *The Ecumenist* 2 (1964) 99–104.

"Ecumenism and Renewal: The Layman's Role." *Way* 20 (October 1964) 28–39. (Interview by T. Mangan.)

"Ecumenism at the Vatican Council." *The Ecumenist* 2 (1964) 21–23.

"Foreword." to *Ecumenical Theology Today* edited by Gregory Baum. Glen Rock, N.J.: Paulist Press, Deus Books, 1964, pp. 7–8.

"A Good Beginning." *Commonweal* 81 (1964) 66–68.

"*Honest to God* and Traditional Theology." *The Ecumenist* 2 (1964) 65–68.

"How Anti-Semitism Found a Home in Christian Teaching." Review of *The Teaching of Contempt* by Jules Isaac. New York: Holt, Rinehart, & Winston, 1964, in *Commonweal* 80 (1964) 372–373.

"Is the Church's Position on Birth Control Infallible?" *The Ecumenist* 2 (1964) 83–85.

"The Meaning of Ecumenism." *Catholic Mind* 62 (1964) 22–29.

"Mid-Point in the Session." *Commonweal* 81 (1964) 191–194.

"The Multiplication of Masses." *The Ecumenist* 3 (1964) 7–9, 12. [Reprinted in *Ecumenical Theology No. 2* edited by Gregory Baum (1967).]

"A Note on Ecumenism at Vatican II." *The Ecumenist* 3 (1964) 1–3.

"Report From Rome." *Commonweal* 82 (1964). (See every other issue from 9 October to 11 December.)

"Theological Reflections on the Second Vatican Council." in *Ecumenical Dialogue at Harvard: The Roman Catholic-Protestant Colloquium* edited by Samuel H. Miller and G. Ernst Wright. Cambridge, Massachusetts: Harvard University Press, 1964, pp. 71–90.

"The Theology of the Blessed Virgin Mary and the Council." *The Ecumenist* 2 (1964) 33–36. [Reprinted in *Ecumenical Theology Today* edited by Gregory Baum (1964).]

"Triumphs and Failures." *Commonweal* 81 (1964) 377–381.

"What the Vatican Council Could Do for the Jews." in *Ecumenical Theology Today* edited by Gregory Baum. Glen Rock. N.J.: Paulist Press, Deus Books, 1964, pp. 226–236.

"Why There Was a Council." *North American Liturgical Week* 25 (1964) 3–9.

1965

"Birth Control: What Happened?" *Commonweal* 83 (1965) 369–371; Replies 83 (1966) 542–543, 571ff., 84 (1966) 3ff.; and Rejoinder 84 (1966) 128.

"The Christian Adventure: Risk and Renewal." *The Furrow* 16 (1965) 336–352; Replies 440–445, 503–506; and Rejoinder 570–572. [Reprinted in *The Critic* 23 (April-May 1965) 40–53.]

"Collaboration: A Pastoral Problem." *The Ecumenist* 3 (1965) 42–45. [Reprinted in *Ecumenical Theology No. 2* edited by Gregory Baum (1967).]

"Commentary on *De Ecclesia*." in *The Constitution on the*

Church of Vatican Council II edited by Edward H. Peters with a foreword by Abbot Basil C. Butler. Glen Rock, N.J.: Paulist Press, Deus Books, 1965, pp. 15–60.

"The Constitution on the Church." *Journal of Ecumenical Studies* 2 (1965) 1–30.

"Doctrinal Renewal." *Journal of Ecumenical Studies* 2 (1965) 365–381. [Reprinted in *Ecumenical Theology No. 2* edited by Gregory Baum (1967).]

"The Ecclesial Reality of the Other Churches." in *The Church and Ecumenism. Concilium,* vol. 4. Edited by Hans Küng. New York: Paulist Press, 1965, pp. 62–86. [Reprinted in *Ecumenical Theology No. 2* edited by Gregory Baum (1967).]

"The Final Session: Off to a Good Start." *Commonweal* 83 (1965) 52–55.

"Five Decrees." *Commonweal* 83 (1965) 237–240.

"Foreword" to *Churchmen in Dialogue.* Toronto: The Canadian Register, 1965, pp. 9–12. (A project of the Canadian Council of Christians and Jews and the Canadian Register.)

"Foundation of Religious Liberty: Dignity and Destiny of Man." *The Basilian Teacher* 9 (1965) 381–385.

"Indulgences—An Exchange of Letters." *The Ecumenist* 3 (1965) 79–81. (With J. R. Sheets.)

"Indulgences at the Council." *Commonweal* 83 (1965) 307ff.

"The Manifold Presence of Christ at Mass." *The Ecumenist* 3 (1965) 69–72. [Reprinted in *Ecumenical Theology No. 2* edited by Gregory Baum (1967).]

"The Ministerial Priesthood." *The Ecumenist* 4 (1965) 4–7. [Reprinted in *Christian Unity Digest* 1 (March 1966) 23–24; and in *Ecumenical Theology No. 2* edited by Gregory Baum (1967).]

"On the Modern World: The Council Discussion of Schema 13 and of the Jews." *Commonweal* 83 (1965) 117–120.

"Peace, Priests and the Missions: Report From the Council." *Commonweal* 83 (1965) 175–178.

"The Pope's Letter." *Way* 21 (1965) 29–37.

"Silence on Indulgences." *The Ecumenist* 3 (1965) 37–39. [Reprinted in *Ecumenical Theology No. 2* edited by Gregory Baum (1967).]

"Teaching Authority of Vatican II." *The Ecumenist* 3 (1965) 89–93. [Reprinted in *Saint Columban's Review* 4 (1966) 20–28; and in *Ecumenical Theology No. 2* edited by Gregory Baum (1967).]

"The Tentative Text on Jewish-Christian Relations." *The Ecumenist* 3 (1965) 56–59.

1966

"Catholics May Use Contraceptives Now." *The Globe Magazine. The Globe and Mail* (9 April 1966) 6–7.

"Christianity and Other Religions: A Catholic Problem." *Cross Currents* 16 (1966) 447–462.

"Commentary on *Decretum De Accommodata Renovatione Vitae Religiosae.*" in *The Decree on the Renewal of Religious Life of Vatican Council II* translated by Austin Flannery. New York: Paulist Press, Deus Books, 1966, pp. 9–55.

"The Conciliar Statement on the Jews." *The Ecumenist* 4 (1966) 27–29. [Reprinted in *Ecumenical Theology No. 2* edited by Gregory Baum (1967).]

"The Council Ends." *Commonweal* 83 (1966) 402–405.

"Declaration on Religious Freedom: Development of Its Doctrinal Basis." *The Ecumenist* 4 (1966) 121–126. [Reprinted in *Ecumenical Theology No. 2* edited by Gregory Baum (1967).]

"The Doctrine on Revelation at Vatican Council II." *The Ecumenist* 4 (1966) 24–26. [Reprinted in *Christian Unity Digest* 1 (November 1966) 32–33; and in *Ecumenical Theology No. 2* edited by Gregory Baum (1967).]

"Does God Punish?" *The Ecumenist* 5 (1966) 7–10. [Reprinted in *Pastoral Life* 15 (1967) 225–230; and in *Does God Punish?* edited by Richard McCarthy. New York: Paulist Press, Deus Books, 1968, pp. 11–21.]

"Introduction." to *The Teachings of the Second Vatican Council: Complete Texts of the Constitutions, Decrees, and Declarations.* Westminster, Maryland: The Newman Press, 1966, pp. vii–xi.

"Die Konstitution *De Divina Revelatione.*" *Catholica, Vierteljahresschrift für Kontroverstheologie* 20 (1966) 85–107.

"Mixed Marriage: An Ecumenical Issue." *The Ecumenist* 4 (1966) 73–76. [Reprinted in *Ecumenical Theology No. 2* edited by Gregory Baum (1967).]

"The Protestant Response to the Council." *Journal of Ecumenical Studies* 3 (1966) 360–362.

"Relationship of the Church to Judaism." in *Vatican II and the Jews.* London: Centre for Biblical and Jewish Studies, 1966, pp. 9–17.

"*Sensus Fidelium:* The Role of the Laity in the Development of Doctrine." *Pax Romana Journal* 10 (1966) 9–13.

"Two Postscripts on Interpreting *Mysterium Fidei.*" *Social Justice Review* 59 (1966) 214–215.

"Vatican II and Catholic-Orthodox Dialogue." *Diakonos* 2 (1966) 14–21.

"Viewpoints on LSD." *Ave Maria* 104 (17 December 1966) 11–13. (With Fredric Wertham.)

"The Voice and the Crowd." in *Media 1.* Toronto: CBC Publications, 1966, pp. 12–18. (A dialogue with Northrop Frye.) [Portions reprinted under the title "A Dialogue on Man's Search for Salvation." *The Varsity Graduate* (University of Toronto) 13 (1966) 75–76.]

"Witness to Divine Reality." *The Christian Century* 83 (1966) 427–429. [Reprinted in *Christian Unity Digest* 1 (June 1966) 31–32; and in *Frontline Theology* edited by Dean Peerman. Richmond, Virginia: John Knox Press, 1967, pp. 94–100.]

1967
"Catholic Doctrinal Continuity and Change." *Insight* 6 (Fall 1967) 43–51.

"The Church in the World." in *Ecumenical Theology No. 2* edited by Gregory Baum. Glen Rock, N.J.: Paulist Press, Deus Books, 1967, pp. 182–208.

"Commentary on *De Ecclesia In Mundo Huius Temporis.*" in *The Pastoral Constitution on the Church in the Modern World of Vatican Council II* with a second commentary by Donald Campion. Glen Rock, N.J.: Paulist Press, Deus Books, 1967, pp.1–77.

"*Communication in Sacris* in the Decree on Ecumenism." *One in Christ* 3 (1967) 417–428.

"The Doctrinal Basis for Jewish-Christian Dialogue." *Dialog* 6 (1967) 200–209. [Reprinted in *The Month* 38 (1967) 232–245; and in *The Ecumenist* 6 (1968) 145–152.]

"Ecumenism After Vatican Council II." in *Oecumenica 1967* edited by F. W. Kantzenbach and V. Vajta. Minneapolis: Augsburg Publishing House, 1967, pp. 149–169.

"Ecumenism at Toronto." *The Ecumenist* 5 (1967) 81–93. [Reprinted in *Christian Unity Digest* 3 (January 1968) 5–9.]

"Foreword." to *Ecumenical Theology No. 2* edited by Gregory Baum, Glen Rock, N.J.: Paulist Press, Deus Books, 1967, pp. 1–2.

"Foreword." to *Infallibility of the Laity: The Legacy of Newman* by Samuel D. Femiano. New York: Herder and Herder, 1967, pp. ix-xiii.

Review of *The Future of Belief* by Leslie Dewart. New York: Herder and Herder, 1967, in *Catholic World* 204 (1967) 309–312.

"Introducing Four Reviews of Dewart's *Future of Belief.*" *The Ecumenist* 5 (1967) 17–19.

"Introduction." to *The Future of Belief Debate* edited by Gregory Baum. New York: Herder and Herder, 1967, pp. 7–8.

"Laying Foundations for a Theology of Renewal." *Commonweal* 86 (1967) 564–565.

"Liturgy and Unity." *The Ecumenist* 6 (1967) 97–100.

"The Magisterium in a Changing Church." in *Man as Man & Believer. Concilium*, vol. 21. Edited by Edward Schillebeeckx and Boniface Willems. New York: Paulist Press, 1967, pp. 67–83.

"Man in History: The Anthropology of Vatican II." in *The New Morality: Continuity and Discontinuity* edited by William Dunphy. New York: Herder and Herder 1967, pp. 157–173.

"The Mystery of Salvation Is Celebrated in the Church." *National Catholic Reporter* 3 (25 January 1967) 6.

"Orthodoxy Recast." in *The Future of Belief Debate* edited by Gregory Baum. New York: Herder and Herder, 1967, pp. 103–108.

"The Question of Infallibility." *Journal of Ecumenical Studies* 4 (1967) 124–125.

"Reflection on Councils of Churches." *One in Christ* 3 (1967) 159–164.

"Les relations d'Israël et de l'Église." in *L'Église de Vatican II* edited by G. Barauna. Paris: Éditions du Cerf, 1967 (*Unam Sanctum* No. 5lb) pp. 639–650.

"Reopen the Question of Anglican Orders?" *Journal of Ecumenical Studies* 4 (1967) 716–717.

"Restlessness in the Church." *The Ecumenist* 5 (1967) 33–36. [Reprinted in *Christian Unity Digest* 2 (June 1967) 6–7.]

"The Self-Understanding of the Roman Catholic Church at Vatican II." in *The Church in the Modern World: Essays in Honour of James Sutherland Thomson* edited by George Johnston and Wolfgang Roth. Toronto: The Ryerson Press, 1967, pp. 86–107.

"The Synod of Bishops." *Catholic Mind* 65 (1967) 2–4.

"Turning New Leaves." Review of *The Future of Belief* by Leslie Dewart. New York: Herder and Herder, 1967; in *The Canadian Forum* 46 (1967) 234–236.

"Vatican II's Constitution on Revelation: History and Interpretation." *Theological Studies* 28 (1967) 51–75.

1968

"Bishop Simons and Development of Doctrine." *The Ecumenist* 7 (1968) 6–7, 10–12.

"Catholic? Protestant?—or Christian? State of the Question." *America* 118 (1968) 15–16.

"The Church Needs a Theology of Conflict." *U.S. Catholic* 34 (December 1968) 18–20.

"Ecclesiological Commentary on *Humanae Vitae.*" *The Ecumenist* 6 (1968) 180–185.

"Foreword." to *Sexuality and Moral Responsibility* by Robert P. O'Neil and Michael A. Donovan. Washington, D.C.: Corpus Books, 1968, pp. v–vii.

"Freedom of Faith and the Teaching Authority of the Church." *Christian Unity Digest* 3 (March 1968) 19–20.

"A New Creed." *The Ecumenist* 6 (1968) 164–167.

"The New Encyclical on Contraception." *The Homiletic and Pastoral Review* 68 (1968) 1001–1004.

"The Open Church in the Liturgy—An Exchange of Letters." *The Ecumenist* 6 (1968) 138–139. (With Bernard J. Mahoney.)

Review of *A Question of Conscience* by Charles Davis. London: Hodder and Stoughton, 1967, in *Frontier* 11 (1968) 61–64.

"Religion and Prejudice." *The Ecumenist* 6 (1968) 167–171.

"Religion and Psychiatry: Dialogue at St. Michael's College." *The Ecumenist* 6 (1968) 132–136.

"The Right to Dissent." *Commonweal* 88 (1968) 553–554. [Reprinted in *The Catholic Case for Contraception* edited by Daniel Callahan. New York: The Macmillan Company, 1969, pp. 71–76.]

"A Roman Catholic Reaction." *The Ecumenist* 6 (1968) 123–125.

"A Sign of the Times." *Journal of Ecumenical Studies* 5 (1968) 572–573.

"Somerville's Blondel." Review of *Total Commitment: Blondel's "L'Action"* by James Somerville. Washington, D.C.: Corpus Books, 1968; in *Continuum* 6 (1968) 119–122.

"Die Theologische Grundlage für den Jüdisch-Christlicher Dialog." *Orientierung* 32 (1968) 31–38.

1969

"Anglican-Roman Catholic Relations: The New Situation." in *Lambeth Essays on Unity: Essays Written for the Lambeth Conference 1968* edited by Archbishop of Canterbury, Michael Cantuar. London: S.P.C.K., 1969, pp. 44–53.

"A Catholic Response." *The Ecumenist* 7 (1969) 90–92. [Reprinted with the title: "We Are Born in Ambiguity and We Never Totally Escape It." in *Sexuality on the Island Earth* introduced by John J. Kirvan. New York: Paulist Press, 1970, pp. 36–45.]

Review of *Do We Need the Church?* by Richard McBrien. New York: Harper & Row, 1969; in *The Ecumenist* 7 (1969) 63–64.

"The Mackay Report." *The Ecumenist* 7 (1969) 57–61.

"The New Ecclesiology." *Commonweal* 91 (1969) 123–128. [Reply by D. Callahan 91 (1969) 128–129.]

"The Papacy." *Catholic World* 209 (1969) 64–66.

"Personal Testimony to Sociology." *The Ecumenist* 8 (1969) 1–4.

Review of *Quest for Past and Future: Essays in Jewish Theology* by Emil L. Fackenheim. Bloomington, Indiana: Indiana University Press, 1968; in *The Ecumenist* 7 (1969) 47–48.

"*The Religions* In Contemporary Roman Catholic Theology." *The Journal of Religious Thought* 26 (1969) 41–56.

"Reply to Bishop Simons." *The Ecumenist* 7 (1969) 46.

"Response to Pinnington." *Journal of Ecumenical Studies* 6 (1969) 414–418.

"Suenens Crying in the Wilderness." *Catholic World* 210 (1969) 103–107.

"Tensions in the Catholic Church." *The Ecumenist* 7 (1969) 21–23, 26.

"Where Is Theology Going?" *The Ecumenist* 7 (1969) 33–36.

1970

"An Answer to Father Tavard." *Journal of Ecumenical Studies* 7 (1970) 788–790.

"Are We Losing the Faith?" *U.S. Catholic* 35 (July 1970) 6–9. (Interview by E. Watkin.)

"Co-Responsibility: A Symposium." *The Ecumenist* 8 (1970) 43–47.

Review of *Divine Humanness* by Aarne Siirala. Philadelphia: Fortress Press, 1970; in *The Ecumenist* 8 (1970) 83–85.

"Does the World Remain Disenchanted?" *Social Research* 37 (1970) 153–202.

"The Future at Brussels." *Catholic World* 212 (1970) 137–140.

"The Institutional Hang-up." *Commonweal* 92 (1970) 212–213.

Review of *Is the Last Supper Finished?* by Arthur A. Vogel. New York: Sheed & Ward, 1968; in *The Ecumenist* 8 (1970) 103–104.

"My Friend God the Politician: God Used to be the Principle of Stability, Now He is the Principle of Change." *The Globe Magazine. The Globe and Mail* (27 June 1970) 8–9.

"The Presence of the Church in Society." *Catholic Mind* 68 (1970) 35–41.

"Prospective Theology." *The Ecumenist* 8 (1970) 72–75.

"Theology and Ideology." *The Ecumenist* 8 (1970) 25–31.

"Toward a New Catholic Theism." *The Ecumenist* 8 (1970) 53–61.

"Vatican II and the Reinterpretation of Doctrine." *The Ecumenist* 9 (1970) 1–4.

"World Congress at Brussels: Liberation." *The Ecumenist* 8 (1970) 94–99.

1971

"The Bible as Norm." *The Ecumenist* 9 (1971) 71–77.

"Catholicism for the U.S.: Develop the Pagan Side." *National Catholic Reporter* 7 (2 April 1971) 16.

"Christian Theology in a Religion Department." *The Ecumenist* 10 (1971) 1–6.

Review of *Contemporary Theology and Psychotherapy* by Thomas A. Oden. Philadelphia: Westminster Press, 1967; in *The Ecumenist* 9 (1971) 29–30.

"Controversy on the God Problem: Reply and Explanation." *The Ecumenist* 9 (1971) 16–22.

"Divine Transcendence." in *The God Experience: Essays in Hope* by Joseph P. Whelan. New York: The Newman Press, 1971, pp. 120–136.

"Does Morality Need the Church?" in *Proceedings of the Catholic Theological Society of America,* vol. 25. Edited by Luke Salm. New York: CTSA, 1971, pp. 159–173. (Conference held in 1970.)

"Earl Neiman: A Great Artist." *Catholic World* 213 (1971) 69–74.

"Editorial Remark on Hans Küng." *Journal of Ecumenical Studies* 8 (1971) 870–871.

"Evil: Where Does It Reside." *National Catholic Reporter* 8 (12 November 1971) 9.

"Faith: Spirit-Created Openness." *National Catholic Reporter Supplement* 7 (28 May 1971) 3ff.

"Infallibility Beyond Polemics." *Commonweal* 94 (1971) 103–105. [Reply by H. Küng 94 (1971) 326–330.]

"One Way of Looking at Catholic Schools." *U.S. Catholic* 36 (December 1971) 40.

"Political Theology Painful for West." *National Catholic Reporter Supplement* 7 (27 August 1971) 11.

"Die Präsenz der Kirche in der Gesellschaft." in *Die Zukunft der*

Kirche: Berichtband des Concilium-Kongresses hrsg. Edward Schillebeeckx. Zurich: Benziger Verlag, 1971, pp. 97–105. (Congress held in 1970.)

"Propositions Are Not Salvational." *National Catholic Reporter* 7 (30 April 1971) 17.

"Religious Experience and Doctrinal Statement." in *New Dimensions in Religious Experience, Proceedings of the College Theology Society* edited by George Divine. New York: Alba House, 1971, pp. 3–11.

"Reply to Rosemary Ruether." *The Ecumenist* 9 (1971) 93–95.

"Science and Commitment: Historical Truth According to Ernst Troeltsch." *Journal of Philosophy of the Social Sciences* 1 (1971) 259–277. [Reprinted in *The Social Imperative* by Gregory Baum (1979).]

"Styles of Theological Reflection for the Future." *Theology Today* 28 (1971) 354–359.

Review of *A Survey of Catholic Theology—1800–1970* by T. M. Schoof. New York: The Newman Press, 1970; in *The Ecumenist* 9 (1971) 31–32.

Review of *The Survival of Dogma: Faith, Authority, and Dogma in a Changing World* by Avery Dulles. Garden City, N.Y.: Doubleday, 1971; in *Theological Studies* 32 (1971) 507–508.

"Synod's Double Message." *National Catholic Reporter* 8 (10 December 1971) 8.

"The Tragic Crisis in East Pakistan." *National Catholic Reporter* 7 (8 October 1971) 13.

"Truth in the Church—Küng, Rahner, and Beyond." *The Ecumenist* 9 (1971) 33–48. [Reprinted in *The Infallibility Debate* edited by John J. Kirvan. New York: Paulist Press, 1971, pp. 1–33.]

"Why Should Marriage Be Normative?" *National Catholic Reporter Supplement* 7 (2 July 1971) 6ff.

"The World's Challenge to the Church." *Sister Formation Bulletin* 17 (Fall 1971) 7–10.

1972

"A Christian Power Game." *National Catholic Reporter* 8 (11 February 1972) 9.

"Contemporary American Romanticism: A Response." in *Man in a New Society. Concilium,* vol. 75. Edited by Franz Böckle. New York: Herder and Herder, 1972, pp. 134–142.

"The Convictions of Others." *The Ecumenist* 10 (1972) 49–52.

"Cultural Causes for the Change of the God Question." in *New Questions on God. Concilium,* vol. 76. Edited by Johann-Baptist Metz. New York: Herder and Herder, 1972, pp. 48–57.

"Ecumenism and the War." *The Ecumenist* 10 (1972) 84–88.

"Eucharistic Hospitality." *The Ecumenist* 11 (1972) 11–16.

"Evolved, Not Revealed." *National Catholic Reporter* 8 (17 March 1972) 16.

"Free Ministry in the U.S.A." in *The Plurality of Ministries. Concilium.* vol. 74. Edited by Hans Küng and Walter Kasper. New York: Herder and Herder, 1972, pp. 146–150.

"Is This Trend a Withdrawal?" *National Catholic Reporter* 9 (8 December 1972) 14.

"The Jews, Faith and Ideology." *The Month* 5 (1972) 176–179. [Reprinted in *The Ecumenist* 10 (1972) 71–76; Reply by C. Forman, 11 (1973) 41–43; and Rejoinder 11 (1973) 44–46.]

"Man's Deepest Response to Evil Is Religious." *The Toronto Star* (5 February 1972) 73.

"New Phase of Christian Renewal." *National Catholic Reporter* 8 (7 April 1972) 11.

"Open Dialogue: Recalling Its Limits." *National Catholic Reporter* 8 (14 January 1972) 11.

"Pastoral Psychology: The Future." *The Journal of Pastoral Counseling* 7 (1972) 60–68.

"Pentecostals Threaten Ecumenism." *National Catholic Reporter* 8 (9 June 1972) 9.

"Religious Teaching Guided by Models in the Imagination." *Imagine: A Journal in Religious Education* 2 (1972) 7–11.

"Rome's Grip Should Be Loosened." *National Catholic Reporter* 9 (10 November 1972) 8.

"Tendenzen in der Katholischen Sexualmoral." *Orientierung* 36 (1972) 270–273.

"We Are Not the People We Used to Be." *New Catholic World* 215 (1972) 244–245, 281.

Review of *What Can You Say About God?* by William A. Luijpen. New York: Paulist Press, 1971; in *The Ecumenist* 10 (1972) 32.

"Why Can't U.S. Jews Be Self-Critical?" *National Catholic Reporter* 8 (29 September 1972) 6ff.

1973

"Abortion: An Ecumenical Dilemma." *Commonweal* 99 (1973) 231–235. [Reprinted in *Bioethics* edited by Thomas Shannon, New York: Paulist Press, 1976, pp. 25–34; and in *Abortion: The Moral Issues* edited by Edward Batchelor, Jr. New York: The Pilgrim Press, 1982, pp. 38–47.]

"Alienation from Religion." *The School Guidance Worker* 28 (1973) 19–22.

"Catholic Sexual Morality: A New Start." *The Ecumenist* 11 (1973) 33–38.

"The Church Moves Left in Spain." *National Catholic Reporter* 9 (22 June 1973) 9.

"Defensive Defense." *National Catholic Reporter* 9 (3 August 1973) 8.

"Dieu a-t-il besoin des eglises?" dans *L'Incroyance au Québec: Approches phénoménologiques, théologiques et pastorales. Collection de Théologie: Héritage et Projet,* vol. 7. A. Charron, G.-M. Bertrand, et R. Laurin, en collaboration. Montréal: Fidés, 1973, pp. 213–220.

"Église et Politique." *Relations* 381 (1973) 118–121.

"Eschatology." *Chicago Studies* 12 (1973) 304–311. [Reprinted in *An American Catholic Catechism* edited by George J. Dyer. New York: The Seabury Press, 1975, pp. 89–97.]

"Evil Is Both Personal and Institutional." *National Catholic Reporter* 9 (9 March 1973) 9.

"Foreword." to *The New Agenda* by Andrew Greeley. Garden City, N.Y.: Doubleday, 1973, pp. 11–34. [Reprinted with the title, "The Theology of Andrew Greeley." *The Ecumenist* 11 (1973) 85–90.]

"The Future of Catholic Theology." *National Catholic Reporter* 9 (5 January 1973) 11.

"Harvey Cox' *Seduction*." Review of *The Seduction of the Spirit* by Harvey Cox. New York: Simon and Schuster, 1973; in *Commonweal* 99 (1973) 22–23.

"Holy Sexuality." *The Month* 6 (1973) 104–108.

"Ministry in the Church." *The Ecumenist* 11 (1973) 76–80. [Reprinted in *Women and Orders* edited by Roger J. Heyer. New York: Paulist Press, 1974, pp. 57–66.]

"Mission and Power: A Reply." *The Ecumenist* 11 (1973) 44–46.

"Sociologists Look at Religion." *The Ecumenist* 11 (1973) 61–64.

"Survival of Canada and the Christian Church." *The Ecumenist* 11 (1973) 23–28.

"The Survival of the Sacred." in *The Persistence of Religion. Concilium,* vol. 81. Edited by Gregory Baum and Andrew Greeley. New York: Herder and Herder, 1973, pp. 11–22.

"Theological Pluralism Important." *National Catholic Reporter* 9 (26 January 1973) 8.

1974

"Catholic Homosexuals." *Commonweal* 99 (1974) 479–482. [Reprinted in *Homosexuality and Ethics* edited by Edward Batchelor, Jr. New York: The Pilgrim Press, 1980, pp. 22–27.]

"Continuing the Discussion: The Jewish-Christian Dialogue." *Christianity and Crisis* 34 (1974) 295–297.

"A Dialogue: Christian-Jewish Relations in Today's World." *Religious Education* 69 (1974) 132–149. (With W. Gunther Plaut.)

"The Dynamic Conscience." *The Ecumenist* 12 (1974) 61–64. [Reply by A. Ambrozic and Rejoinder under the title, "An Exchange of Letters." *The Ecumenist* 13 (1974) 12–15.]

"Editorial." in *The Church As Institution. Concilium,* vol. 91. Edited by Gregory Baum and Andrew Greeley. New York: Herder and Herder, 1974, pp. 7–8.

"Faith After Auschwitz—and Belfast." *Commonweal* 101 (1974) 153–159.

Review of *Faith After the Holocaust* by Eliezer Berkovits. New York: Ktav, 1973; in *Sidic* 7 (1974) 42–43.

"Infallibility on Trial." *The Ecumenist* 12 (1974) 95–96.

"Introduction." to *Faith and Fratricide* by Rosemary Ruether. New York: The Seabury Press, 1974, pp. 1–22.

"Les mutations de la foi chrétienne." dans *Les mutations de la foi chrétienne. Collection "Foi et Liberté."* Montréal: Fidés, 1974, pp. 51–75, 91–101. (Conférences prononcées à l'occasion des Journées universitaires de la Pensée chrétienne, Octobre 1973, à l'Université de Montréal.)

"The Pluralism of Truth in Scheler and Mannheim." in *Le Pluralisme: Symposium interdisciplinaire/Pluralism: Its Meaning Today. Collection de Théologie: Héritage et Projet,* vol. 10. I. Beaubien, C. Davis , G. Langerin, & R. Lapointe, en collaboration. Montréal: Fidés, 1974, pp. 251–272.

"Response to Charles Davis." *Studies in Religion/Sciences Religieuses* 4 (1974) 222–224.

"Rome Unrealistic on Küng Position." *National Catholic Reporter* 11 (8 November 1974) 14.

"Schools, Values and the Future." in *Schools: Their Value to the Community. Proceedings of the 1974 Conference of the Ontario Educational Association.* Toronto: O.I.S.E., 1974, pp. 42–46.

"Sociology and Theology." in *The Church as Institution. Conci-*

lium, vol. 91. Edited by Gregory Baum and Andrew Greeley. New York: Herder and Herder, 1974, pp. 22–31.

"Theology After Auschwitz: A Conference Report." *The Ecumenist* 12 (1974) 65–80. (Theological symposium held at the Cathedral of St. John the Divine, New York City, 1974.) [Reprinted in *The Social Imperative* by Gregory Baum (1979).]

"Unity or Renewal?" *The Ecumenist* 13 (1974) 5–9.

"The University and the Christian." *Queen's Quarterly* 81 (1974) 20–27.

1975

"Canadian Scholars Affirm Solidarity With Israel." *National Catholic Reporter* 11 (31 January 1975) 9.

"The Christian Left at Detroit: Theology in the Americas." *The Ecumenist* 13 (1975) 81–100. [Reprinted in *Theology in the Americas* edited by S. Torres and J. Eagleson, Maryknoll, New York: Orbis Books, 1976, p. 399–429; and in *The Social Imperative* by Gregory Baum (1979).]

"An Ecclesiological Principle." in *No Famine in the Land: Studies in Honor of John L. McKenzie* edited by James W. Flanagan and Anita Weisbrod Robinson. Missoula, Montana: Scholars Press for the Institute For Antiquity and Christianity—Claremont, 1975, pp. 263–274.

Review of *Freud and Original Sin* by Sharon MacIsaac. New York: Paulist Press, 1974; in *The Ecumenist* 13 (1975) 45–47.

"The Impact of Sociology on Catholic Theology." in *Proceedings of the Catholic Theological Society of America,* vol. 30. Edited by Luke Salm. New York: CTSA, 1975, pp. 1–29. [Reprinted in *The Social Imperative* by Gregory Baum (1979).]

"Introduction" to *Journeys: The Impact of Personal Experience on Religious Thought* edited by Gregory Baum. New York: Paulist Press, 1975, pp. 1–4.

"The New Agenda." Review of *The New Agenda* by Andrew Greeley. Garden City, N.Y.: Doubleday, 1973; in *Frontier* 18 (1975) 176–178.

"Personal Experience and Styles of Thought." in *Journeys: The Impact of Personal Experience on Religious Thought* edited by Gregory Baum. New York: Paulist Press, 1975, pp. 5–33.

"Salvation Is From the Jews: A Story of Prejudice." in *Disputation and Dialogue: Readings in Jewish-Christian Encounter* edited by F. E. Talmage. New York: KTAV Publishing House, 1975, pp. 313–319.

"La vocation des intellectuels dans l'Église." dans *Les Intellectuels dans L'Église. Concilium,* 101. Edited by Gregory Baum and Andrew Greeley. Paris: Éditions Beauchesne, 1975, pp. 27–36.

1976

Review of *Against the World for the World* edited by Richard J. Neuhaus. New York: The Seabury Press, 1976; in *The New Review of Books and Religion* 1 (1976) 8.

Review of *Blessed Rage for Order: The New Pluralism in Theology* by David Tracy. New York: The Seabury Press, 1975; in *The Critic* 34 (Summer 1976) 71–74.

"The College: A Thinking Community." *The Ecumenist* 14 (1976) 45–48.

"Éditorial." dans *Les Femmes dans L'Église. Concilium.* 111. Edited by Gregory Baum and Andrew Greeley. Paris: Éditions Beauchesne, 1976, pp. 7–9.

"Joe Burton: Catholic and Saskatchewan Socialist." *The Ecumenist* 14 (1976) 70–77.

"Liberation Theology: First the Theory ... Then Justice." *National Catholic Reporter* 12 (8 October 1976) 8–9.

"Messianic Misconception." Review of *Karl Marx's Philosophy of Man* by John Plamenatz. Oxford: Clarendon Press, 1976; in *The Canadian Forum* 51 (1976) 60–61.

"New Intellectuals." *The Tablet* 230 (1976) 116–117ff.

Review of *On Becoming a Musical Mystical Bear* by Matthew Fox. New York: Paulist Press, 1976; in *The Ecumenist* 15 (1976) 13–14.

"Prayer and Society." in *Emerging Issues in Religious Education* edited by G. Durka and J. Smith. New York: Paulist Press, 1976, pp. 18–28.

"Religion and Capitalism According to Bell." *The Ecumenist* 14 (1976) 59–62.

"Secular Spiritualities: Alcoholics Anonymous, Therapies, Radical Politics." *New Catholic World* 219 (1976) 52–57.

"Theological Reflection on *Maker of Heaven and Earth.*" in *Christian Theology: A Case Study Approach* edited by R. A. Evans and Thomas D. Parker. New York: Harper & Row, 1976, pp. 83–88.

Contributions to *Theology in the Americas* edited by S. Torres and J. Eagleson. Maryknoll, N.Y.: Orbis Books, 1976, pp. 87–89, 390–391.

1977

"Alienation and Reconciliation: A Socio-Theological Approach." in *From Alienation to At-One-Ness. Proceedings of the Theology Institute of Villanova University* edited by Francis A. Eigo. Villanova, Pennsylvania: Villanova University Press, 1977, pp. 133–170.

"The Ambiguity of Biblical Religion." *Theology Today* 33 (1977) 344–353.

"Canadian Socialism and the Christian Church." in *Christianity and Socialism. Concilium,* vol. 105. Edited by Johann-Baptist Metz and Jean-Pierre Jossua. New York: The Seabury Press, 1977, pp. 13–22.

"Conference Calls Canadians to New Images of the Church." *Catholic New Times* 1 (27 March 1977) 8.

"Crisis and Commitment: The Necessity To Act." in *Humanizing America: A Post-Holocaust Imperative* edited by Josephine Knopp. Philadelphia: Temple University Press, 1977, pp. 89–97. (The Second Philadelphia Conference on the Holocaust.)

"Editorial Summary." in *Ethnicity. Concilium,* vol. 101. Edited by Gregory Baum and Andrew Greeley. New York: The Seabury Press, 1977, pp. 100–102.

"A Look at the Past for the Sake of the Future." in *Proceedings of the 1977 Conference of the Institute for Christian Life in Canada.* Toronto: I.C.L.C., 1977, pp. 27–41. (Mimeographed symposium papers.)

"Moses Coady: Critique of Capitalism." *Chelsea Journal* 3 (1977) 229–231.

"Multiculturalism in Canada." *The Ecumenist* 16 (1977) 10–16. [Reprinted with title, "Multiculturalism and Ethnicity." in *The Social Imperative* by Gregory Baum (1979).]

Review of *On Being a Christian* by Hans Küng. Translated by Edward Quinn. Garden City, N.Y.: Doubleday, 1977; in *The Critic* 35 (Spring 1977) 81–85.

Review of *On Being Human Religiously: Selected Essays in Religion and Society* James Luther Adams. Boston: Beacon Press, 1976; in *The Ecumenist* 15 (1977) 46, 48.

"Political Theology in Canada." *The Ecumenist* 15 (1977) 33–46. [Reprinted in *The Social Imperative* by Gregory Baum (1979).]

"The Pope on Authentic Community." *Catholic New Times* 3 (1 July 1977) 3.

"Reply to A. de Valk's *Christianity, Society and Gregory Baum.*" *Chelsea Journal* 3 (1977) 149–152.

"Rethinking the Church's Mission After Auschwitz." in *Auschwitz: Beginning of a New Era? Reflections on the Holocaust* edited by Eva Fleischner. New York: Ktav, 1977, pp. 113–128.

Review of *Simone Weil: A Life* by Simone Petrement. Translated by R. Rosenthal. New York: Pantheon Books, 1976; in *Queen's Quarterly* 84 (1977) 482–483.

"Social Catholicism in Nova Scotia: The Thirties." in *Religion and Culture in Canada* edited by Peter Slater. Waterloo, Ontario: Canadian Society for the Study of Religion/Wilfred Laurier University Press, 1977, pp. 118–148.

"Socialism and Christianity." Review of *The Social Decision* by Paul Tillich. New York: Harper & Row, 1977; in *The Canadian Forum* 57 (1977) 27–28. [Reprinted in *The Ecumenist* 16 (1978) 62–64.]

"Spirituality and Social Action." in *Proceedings of the 1977 Conference of the Institute for Christian Life in Canada.* Toronto: I.C.L.C., 1977, pp. 62–74. (Mimeographed symposium papers.)

"Theological Method of Segundo's *The Liberation of Theology.*" in *Proceedings of the Catholic Theological Society of America,* vol. 32. Edited by Luke Salm. New York: CTSA, 1977, pp. 120–124.

1978

"Adult Education as a Political Enterprise." *Christian Movement for Peace* 4 (1978) 1–3, 6. [Reprinted in *Learning* 2 (1979) 9–10, 22.]

"Blessed Are the Poor." The Ecumenist 16 (1978) 86–91.

"Canadian Bishops Adapt Liberation Theology." *Cross Currents* 28 (1978) 97–103.

"Canadian Bishops on Social Justice." *The Ecumenist* 16 (1978) 46–47.

"Catholics and Social Action." *The Christian Century* 95 (1978) 347–349.

"Chosenness in Christian Tradition." *The Ecumenist* 17 (1978) 6–11. [Reprinted in *Sidic* 13 (1980) 9–13; French edition: "Le concept d'élection dans la tradition chrétienne." *Sidic* 8 (1980) 9–13.]

"The Contemporary Social Gospel." in *Proceedings of the 1978 Conference of the Institute for Christian Life in Canada.* Toronto: I.C.L.C., 1978, pp. 1–17. (Mimeographed symposium papers.)

"Critical Theology." in *Conversion,* edited by Walter Conn. New York: Alba House, 1978, pp. 281–295.

"Editorial." in *Communication in the Church. Concilium,* vol. 111. Edited by Gregory Baum and Andrew Greeley. New York: The Seabury Press, 1978, pp. vii–viii.

"Foreword." to *Anti-Judaism in Christian Theology* by Charlotte Klein, translated by E. Quinn. Philadelphia: Fortress Press, 1978, pp. ix–xi.

"The French Bishops and Euro-Communism." *The Ecumenist* 16 (1978) 17–25. [Reprinted in *The Social Imperative* by Gregory Baum (1979).]

"German Theologians and Liberation Theology." *The Ecumenist* 16 (1978) 49–51.

"Introduction." to *Searching for Truth: A Personal View of Roman Catholicism* by Peter Kelly. New York: Collins, 1978, pp. 7–13.

"Keeping Up in Christianity." Review of *Protestant and Roman Catholic Ethics* by James M. Gustafson. Chicago: University of Chicago Press, 1978; in *The Canadian Forum* 58 (1978) 30–32.

"Moderating the Catholic Claims." *The Ecumenist* 16 (1978) 70–73.

"Spirituality and Society." *Religious Education* 73 (1978) 266–283. [Reprinted in *The Social Imperative* by Gregory Baum (1979).]

"What Is New in the Bishops' Statement?" *Catholic New Times* 2 (29 January 1978) 8.

1979

"Attack on the New Social Gospel." *The Ecumenist* 17 (1979) 81–84. (Revised version of a lecture given on 4 August 1979 at the Institute of Public Affairs, Geneva Park, Couchiching, Ontario, Canada.)

"Catholic Dogma After Auschwitz." in *AntiSemitism and the Foundations of Christianity* edited by Alan T. Davies. New York: Paulist Press, 1979, pp. 137–150.

"Catholic Foundation of Human Rights." *The Ecumenist* 18 (1979) 6–12.

"The Catholic Press as Organ of Communication." in *The Future of the Catholic Press.* Institute of the Catholic Press. Milwaukee, Wisconsin: Marquette University Press, 1979, pp. 8–11.

"The Christian Left Looking for Allies." *The Canadian Forum* 57 (1979) 6–7. [Reprinted in *Catholic New Times* 3 (15 July 1979) 8.]

"Christianity and Socialism." *Canadian Dimension* 13 (1979) 30–35. [Reprinted with the title: "Religion and Socialism," *The Social Imperative* by Gregory Baum (1979).]

"Conversation with Gabriel Vahanian." *The Ecumenist* 17 (1979) 65–68.

Review of *Facing Up to Modernity* by Peter Berger. New York: Basic Books, 1977; in *The Ecumenist* 17 (1979) 63–64.

"Faithful Wrestling." Review of *Struggle and Fulfillment: The Inner Dynamics of Religion and Morality* by Donald Evans. London: Collins, 1979; in *The Christian Century* 96 (1979) 1190–1191. [Reprinted in *The Ecumenist* 18 (1980) 47–48.

"The First Papal Encyclical." *The Ecumenist* 17 (1979) 55–59.

Review of *God-Wrestling,* by Arthur Waskow. New York: Schocken Books, 1978; in *The Ecumenist* 17 (1979) 92–93.

"Küng and Capitalism." *The Ecumenist* 17 (1979) 46–48.

"Marx and Marxism." *Proceedings of the 1979 Conference of the Institute for Christian Life in Canada.* Toronto: I.C.L.C., 1979, pp. 60–79. (Mimeographed symposium papers.)

"Middle Class Religion in America." in *Christianity and the Bourgeoisie. Concilium,* vol. 125. Edited by Johann-Baptist Metz. New York: The Seabury Press, 1979, pp. 15–23.

"Nationalism and Social Justice." in *The Social Imperative: Essays on the Critical Issues That Confront the Christian Churches* by Gregory Baum. New York: Paulist Press, 1979, pp. 218–230. (Originally given as a public lecture at McGill University, Montreal, May 1977.)

"Pope John Paul's View of Dissent." *The Ecumenist* 17 (1979)

88–89. [French edition: "Le Pape et la dissidence." *Relations* 39 (1979) 250–251.]

"Quebec Bishops Defend Self-Determination." *Catholic New Times* 3 (30 September 1979) 2.

"Sexuality and Critical Enlightenment." in *Dimensions of Human Sexuality* edited by Dennis Doherty. Garden City, N.Y.: Doubleday, 1979, pp. 79–94.

"Sociology as Critical Humanism." in *The Social Imperative: Essays on the Critical Issues That Confront the Christian Churches* by Gregory Baum. New York: Paulist Press, 1979, pp. 148–167. (Originally given as a public lecture at King's College, London, Ontario, November 1976.)

"La solidarité canadienne." dans *Le référendum: un enjeu collectif. Cahiers de recherche éthique,* 7. Montréal: Fides, 1979, pp. 161–165.

"Theology and Canadian Business." *Queen's Quarterly* 85 (1979) 650–653.

"Toward a Gay Christian Ethic." *Insight* 3 (1979) 8–9.

"Values and Society." *The Ecumenist* 17 (1979) 25–31.

1980

"Canadian Christian Professors Respond to Israel's Plans for Jerusalem." *Catholic New Times* 4 (21 September 1980) 9. (With Cranford Pratt, Cyril Powles, Thomas Langan, William Dunphy, Willard Oxtoby, and John Burbidge.)

"The Church's Growing Concern About Social Injustice Is Good Christianity." *Institutions in Crisis, The 48th Annual Couchiching Conference* edited by Dean Walker. Toronto: Yorkminster Publishing, 1980, pp. 127–149.

"Debate Over Utopia." *The Ecumenist* 18 (1980) 60–64.

"Definitions of Religion in Sociology." in *What Is Religion? An Inquiry for Christian Theology. Concilium,* vol. 136. Edited by Mircea Eliade and David Tracy. New York: The Seabury Press, 1980, pp. 25–32.

Review of *Discerning the Way: A Theology of the Jewish-Chris-*

tian Reality by Paul Van Buren. New York: The Seabury Press, 1980; in *Commonweal* 107 (1980) 598–601. [Reprinted in *The Ecumenist* 19 (1981) 51–53.]

"Editorial." in *Work and Religion. Concilium,* vol. 131. Edited by Gregory Baum. New York: The Seabury Press, 1980, pp. vii–viii.

"Introduction." to *Sociology and Human Destiny: Essays on Sociology, Religion, and Society* edited by Gregory Baum. New York: The Seabury Press, Crossroad Books, 1980, pp. ix–xii.

"The Küng Case: Brief Reflections." *The Ecumenist* 18 (1980) 33–34. [Reprinted in *Catholic New Times* 4 (27 January 1980) 9.]

"The Maritime Bishops: Social Criticism." *The Ecumenist* 18 (1980) 35. [Replies by R. Sacouman, T. Langan, and G. Schmitz; 18 (1980) 35–41.]

"The Meaning of Ideology." in *Proceedings of the Catholic Theological Society of America,* vol. 34. Edited by Luke Salm. New York: CTSA, 1980, pp. 171–175. (Conference held in 1979.)

"Moral People, Immoral Society." *The Witness* 63 (1980) 10–13, 17.

"Peter Berger's Unfinished Symphony." in *Sociology and Human Destiny: Essays on Sociology, Religion, and Society* edited by Gregory Baum. New York: The Seabury Press, Crossroad Books, 1980, pp. 110–129. [Reprinted in *Commonweal* 107 (1980) 263–270.]

"A Pope from the Second World." *The Ecumenist* 18 (1980) 22–26.

"Préface." to *De Sodome à L'Exode: Jalons pour une théologie de la libération gaie* by Guy Ménard. Montréal: Les Éditions Univers, Inc., 1980, pp. 11–15.

Review of *Prophets Denied Honor* edited by Antonio Arroyo. Maryknoll, N.Y.: Orbis Books, 1980; in *The Ecumenist* 18 (1980) 95–96.

"Reflections on the Lord's Prayer." *Orbit 51* 11 (1980) 3–4.

"Relevance of the Antigonish Movement Today." *Journal of Canadian Studies/Revue d'études canadiennes* 15 (1980) 110–117.

"The Roman Procedures." *The Ecumenist* 18 (1980) 45–46.

"The Sociology of Roman Catholic Theology." in *Sociology and Theology: Alliance and Conflict* edited by D. Martin, J. O. Mills, and W. S. F. Pickering. London: The Harvester Press, 1980, pp. 120–135.

"Theology in the Americas: Detroit II." *The Ecumenist* 18 (1980) 90–94. [Reprinted in *Journal of Ecumenical Studies* 17 (1980) 750–753.]

1981

Review of *The Analogical Imagination: Christian Theology and the Culture of Pluralism* by David Tracy. New York: Crossroad Books, 1981; in *Religious Studies Review* 7 (1981) 284–290.

Review of *Challenge to the Laity* by Russell Barta. Huntington, Indiana: Our Sunday Visitor, 1980; in *The Ecumenist* 19 (1981) 49–50.

Review of *Christian Religious Education* by Thomas H. Groome. New York: Harper & Row, 1980; in *The Ecumenist* 19 (1981) 79–80.

"A Disappointing Proposal." Review of *Authority* by Richard Sennett. New York: Alfred A. Knopf, 1980; in *Social Policy* (May–June 1981) 59–62.

"Ecumenical Theology: A New Approach." *The Ecumenist* 19 (1981) 65–78.

"Editorial." in *Neo-Conservatism: Social and Religious Phenomenon. Concilium,* vol. 141. Edited by Gregory Baum. New York: The Seabury Press, 1981, pp. vii–viii.

"Encyclical *Overcomes Marxism from Within:* Gregory Baum." *Catholic New Times* 5 (8 November 1981) 3.

"Faith in Progress or Christian Faith?" *The Ecumenist* 19 (1981) 43–48.

"Foreword." to *Struggle and Submission: R. C. Zaehner on Mysticisms* by William Lloyd Newell. Washington, D.C.: University Press of America, 1981, pp. x–xiii.

Review of *Identity and the Sacred* by Hans Mol. New York: The Free Press, 1976; in *The Ecumenist* 19 (1981) 91–93.

"John Paul II's Encyclical on Labor." *The Ecumenist* 20 (1981) 1–4.

"Liberation Theology and *The Supernatural.*" *The Ecumenist* 19 (1981) 81–87.

Review of *Marx Against the Marxists* by Jose Miranda. Maryknoll, N.Y.: Orbis Books, 1980; in *The Ecumenist* 19 (1981) 55–56.

Review of *Marxism: An American Christian Perspective* by Arthur F. McGovern. Maryknoll, N.Y.: Orbis Books, 1980; in *The Ecumenist* 19 (1981) 53–55.

Review of *The Mind of John Paul II* by George H. Williams. New York: The Seabury Press, 1981; in *The Ecumenist* 19 (1981) 56–58.

"Neo-Conservative Critics of the Churches." in *Neo-Conservatism: Social and Religious Phenomenon. Concilium,* vol. 141. Edited by Gregory Baum. New York: The Seabury Press, 1981, pp. 43–50.

"Religious Studies: Faith vs. Science." *Bulletin* (University of Toronto) 14 (23 February 1981) 11.

"Viewsbeat: An Interview with Gregory Baum." *Catalyst for Public Justice* 4 (1981) 12–15.

1982

"L'attitude de l'Église face aux crises économiques." *Communauté Chrétienne* 21 (1982) 43–55.

Review of *The Dream of Christian Socialism* by Bernard Murchland. Washington, D.C.: American Enterprise Institute, 1982; in *The Ecumenist* 20 (1982) 62–64.

"Economics and Religion." *The Ecumenist* 20 (1982) 76–78.

"Editorial." in *The Church and Racism. Concilium,* vol. 151. Edited by Gregory Baum and John Coleman. New York: The Seabury Press, 1982, pp. vii–ix.

Review of *Emmanuel Mounier and the New Catholic Left, 1930–1950* by John Hellman. Toronto: University of Toronto Press, 1982; in *The Ecumenist* 20 (1982) 93–95. [Reprinted with the title: "A Worldly Pascal." *The Canadian Forum* 60 (1982) 30–31.]

"English Speaking Quebecers: Resentment or Justice?" *Catholic New Times* 6 (4 April 1982) 13.

"Franz Werfel's Look at Genocide." in *Through the Sound of Many Voices. Essays in Honor of W. Gunther Plaut's 70th Birthday* edited by Jonathan V. Plaut. Toronto: Lester & Orpen Dennys, 1982, pp. 184–195.

"The Holocaust and Christian Theology." *One World* 20 (1982) 37–40.

"Introduction." to *George Tyrrell & the Catholic Tradition* by Ellen Leonard. London: Darton, Longman and Todd/New York: Paulist Press, 1982, pp. xv–xviii.

"New Jewish Religious Voices." *The Ecumenist* 20 (1982) 81–84.

"New Jewish Religious Voices II." *The Ecumenist* 21 (1982) 6–8.

"New Questions to Psychiatry." *The Bulletin of the National Guild of Catholic Psychiatrists* 28 (1982) 11–18.

Review of *Papal Power* by Jean-Guy Vaillancourt. Berkeley: University of California, 1980; in *The Ecumenist* 20–62.

"The Power of the Poor: Theological and Sociological Perspectives." in *Proceedings of the Catholic Theological Society of America,* vol. 37. Edited by Luke Salm, New York: CTSA, 1982, pp. 165–169.

"Relation entre unité et mission." *Oecuménisme* 66 (1982) 29–30.

"Responses." in *Political Theology in the Canadian Context* edited by Benjamin G. Smillie. Waterloo, Ontario: Wilfrid

Laurier University Press, for the Canadian Corporation for Studies in Religion, 1982, pp. 112, 132–138, 139–141.

"The Retrieval of Subjectivity." *Canadian Journal of Community Mental Health* 1 (1982) 89–102.

"Salvation and Emancipation." *Chicago Studies* 21 (1982) 265–276.

Review of *Solidarity with Victims: Toward a Theology of Social Transformation* by Matthew Lamb. New York: Crossroad Books, 1982; in *Commonweal* 109 (1982) 600–604.

Review of *Spirituality of the Beatitudes* by Michael Crosby. New York: Orbis Books, 1980; in *The Ecumenist* 20 (1982) 79–80.

"Theology Questions Psychiatry: An Address." *The Ecumenist* 20 (1982) 55–59.

1983

"After Twenty Years." *The Ecumenist* 21 (1983) 17–19.

"Canadian Bishops' Economic Reflection Is Model for an Alternative Society." *National Catholic Reporter* 19 (11 March 1983) 10–11.

"Capital, Bishops, and Unemployment." *New Catholic World* 226 (1983) 158–162.

"Gutierrez and the Catholic Tradition." *The Ecumenist* 21 (1983) 81–84.

"The Homosexual Condition and Political Responsibility." in *A Challenge to Love: Gay and Lesbian Catholics in the Church* edited by Robert Nugent. New York: Crossroad Books, 1983, pp. 38–51.

"*Jakob der Lügner* in Christian Perspective." *Seminar: A Journal of Germanic Studies* 19 (1983) 285–288.

Review of *A New Beginning* edited by T. Chu and C. Lind. Toronto: Canadian Council of Churches, 1982; in *The Ecumenist* 22 (1983) 15–16.

"New Jewish Religious Voices III." *The Ecumenist* 21 (1983) 38–41.

"New Jewish Religious Voices IV." *The Ecumenist* 22 (1983) 7–10.

Review of *Religionssoziologie als Kritische Theorie: Die Marxistische Religionskritik und ihre Bedeutung für die Religionssoziologie* by Rainer Neu. Frankfurt: Peter Lang, 1982; in *Religious Studies Review* 9 (1983) 142.

"Should Sin Be Politicized? Gregory Baum's Reply to Darrol Bryant's Proposal." *The Ecumenist* 21 (1983) 54–60.

"Sociology of Religion 1973–1983." in *Twenty Years of "Concilium"—Retrospect and Prospect. Concilium,* vol. 170. Edited by Paul Brand and Edward Schillebeeckx. New York: The Seabury Press, 1983, pp. 1–7.

"La teologia de la liberación y 'sobrenatural'." in *Vida Y Reflexion: Aportes de la teologia de la liberación al pensamiento teológico actual.* Lima, Perú: Centro de Estudios y Publicaciones (CEP), 1983, pp. 59–76.

"Toward a Strategic Theology." Review of *An American Strategic Theology* by John Coleman. New York: Paulist Press, 1982; in *The Ecumenist* 21 (1983) 44–48.

1984

"Being Modern and Medieval, That's John Paul's Charisma." *The Toronto Star* (15 September 1984) B4.

"Beginnings of a Canadian Catholic Social Theory." in *Political Thought in Canada: Contemporary Perspective* edited by Stephen Brooks. Toronto: Irwin Publishing, 1984, pp. 49–80.

Review of *The Bishop of Rome* J. M. R. Tillard. Baltimore: Michael Glazier, 1983; in *The Ecumenist* 22 (1984) 47–48.

Review of *The Bishops and the Bomb* by Jim Castelli. Garden City, N.Y.: Doubleday, 1983; in *The Ecumenist* 22 (1984) 47.

Review of *Canada and the Nuclear Arms Race* edited by Ernie Regehr and Simon Rosenblum. Toronto: James Lorimer & Company, 1983; in *The Ecumenist* 22 (1984) 62–63.

"Canada, Too, Knows Cultural Oppression." *The Prairie Messenger* (22 October 1984) 10–11.

"The Canadian Bishops on the Economic Crisis." *The Furrow* 35 (1984) 487–494.

"Class Struggle and the Magisterium: A New Note." *Theological Studies* 45 (1984) 690–701.

"Dialogue Opening Up to New Dimensions." *National Catholic Reporter* 20 (3 February 1984) 18–19.

"Doctrine sociale de l'Église; corporatisme ou socialisme?" *Études d'économie politique* 1 (September 1984) 13–30.

"Editorial." in *The Sexual Revolution. Concilium.* vol. 173. Edited by Gregory Baum and John Coleman. Edinburgh: T. & T. Clark, 1984, pp. ix–xi.

"Faith and Liberation: Development Since Vatican II." in *Vatican II: Open Questions and New Horizons* edited by Gerald Fagin. Wilmington, Delaware: Michael Glazier, Inc., 1984, pp. 75–104.

Review of *The Growth of the True Church* by Charles Van Engen. New York: Humanities Press, 1981; in *The Ecumenist* 22 (1984) 61–62.

"The Holocaust and Political Theology." in *The Holocaust as Interruption. Concilium,* vol. 175. Edited by Elizabeth Schüssler-Fiorenza and David Tracy. Edinburgh: T. & T. Clark, 1984, pp. 34–42.

"Ideas Need 'Political Will' to Influence." *McMaster News* (May 1984) 8–10.

"Is Ecumenism Threatened in Canada? The Temptation of Triumphalism." *Catholic New Times* 8 (2 September 1984) 11.

"Is God Dead, or Constantine?" Review of *The Politics at God's Funeral* by Michael Harrington. New York: Holt, Rinehart, & Winston, 1983; in *Commonweal* 140 (1984) 89–92.

Review of *Magisterium* by Francis A. Sullivan, S.J. New York: Paulist Press, 1983; in *The Ecumenist* 22 (1984) 63–64.

"Die Option für die Armen. Betrachtungen aus Kanada." in

Glaube im Prozess. Christsein nach dem II. Vaticanum für Karl Rahner. Hrsg. von Elmar Klinger und Klaus Wittstadt. Freiburg: Herder, 1984, pp. 655–665.

"Political Theology in Conflict." *The Ecumenist* 22 (1984) 84–87.

"The Power of Ideas in Society." *The Ecumenist* 23 (1984) 9–14.

"Reactionary or Visionary: The Pope's Visit to Canada." *Our Times* 3 (June 1984) 22–24.

"Should Church Critique of Economy Be Prophetic or Based on 'Consensus'?" *The National Catholic Reporter* 20 (16 March 1984) 16.

Review of *The Spirit of Democratic Capitalism* by Michael Novak. New York: American Enterprise Institute and Simon & Schuster, 1982; in *Religious Studies Review* 10 (1984) 107–112.

"Urgency and Life After Death." Review of *Eternal Life? Life After Death as a Medical, Philosophical, and Theological Problem* by Hans Küng. Translated by Edward Quinn. Garden City, N.Y.: Doubleday, 1984; in *The Globe and Mail* (5 May 1984) 22.

Review of *Vatican II: Open Questions and New Horizons,* edited by Gerald Fagin. Wilmington, Delaware: Michael Glazier, 1984; in *The Ecumenist* 22 (1984) 93.

"The View from Downsview: A Retrospective Look at the Pope in Canada." *Our Times* (November 1984) 42–44.

Review of "War Resistance and Moral Experience." by John R. Mergendoller. Unpublished Doctoral Dissertation. The University of Michigan, 1981; in *Phenomenology + Pedagogy* 2 (1984) 207–210.

1985

"After Liberal Optimism, What?" *Commonweal* 112 (1985) 368–370.

"A Canadian Perspective on the U.S. Pastoral." *Christianity and Crisis* 44 (1985) 516–518. [Reprinted under the title, "Call for Justice: A Comparison." *The Ecumenist* 23 (1985) 43–45.

"The Dawning of Post-Liberal Society." Review of *Religion in the Secular City,* by Harvey Cox. New York: Simon & Schuster, 1984. In *The Ecumenist* 23 (1985) 29–31.

"Dialogue With Evangelicals." In *Justice as Mission: An Agenda for the Church.* Essays in Appreciation of Marjorie and Cyril Powles. Edited by C. Lind and T. Brown. Burlington, Ontario: Trinity Press, 1985, pp. 95–103.

Review of *Eternal Life? Life After Death as a Medical, Philosophical, and Theological Problem,* by Hans Küng. Garden City, N.Y.: Doubleday, 1984. In *The Ecumenist* 23 (1985) 47–48.

Review of *Idols of Our Times,* by Bob Goudzwaard. Downers Grove, Illinois: Inter-Varsity Press, 1984. In *The Ecumenist* 23 (1985) 46–47.

"The Labor Pope in Canada." *The Ecumenist* 23 (1985) 17–23.

"Marxism on the Mind of John Paul II." *National Catholic Reporter* 21 (29 March 1985) 18.

"La nouvelle pensée sociale catholique." *Relations* 45 (1985) 128–130.

"The Witness of Etty Hillesum." *The Ecumenist* 23 (1985) 24–28. [To appear in *Dimensions in the Human Religious Quest,* edited by Joseph Armenti.]

Contributors

Gregory Baum, after many years at St. Michael's College in the University of Toronto, is now Professor of Religious Studies at McGill University, Montreal, PQ.

Robert McAfee Brown is Professor of Theology and Ethics at the Pacific School of Religion, Berkeley, CA. He is the author of numerous books and articles, including *Theology in a New Key: Responding to Liberation Themes* and *Unexpected News: Reading the Bible with Third World Eyes.*

Douglas John Hall is Professor of Christian Theology at McGill University in Montreal. His most recent books are *Imaging God: Dominion as Stewardship* and *God and Human Suffering.*

Mary Ann Hinsdale is Professor of Systematic Theology at Holy Cross College in Worcester, MA. She is a member of the Sisters, Servants of the Immaculate Heart of Mary in Monroe, MI. She was a former doctoral student of Gregory Baum's and has also taught at St. John's Provincial Seminary.

Joe Holland is a founder of the American Catholic Lay Network (ACLN). He has written *The American Journey* and *Social Analysis: Linking Faith and Justice* and spent twelve and one half years in Washington, D.C. at the Center of Concern.

Matthew L. Lamb is Professor of Theology at Boston College. His most recent work is *Solidarity with Victims. Toward a Theology of Social Transformation.*

195

Mary Jo Leddy is the Provincial Coordinator of the North American Province of the Sisters of Sion. A former doctoral student of Gregory Baum's, Mary Jo is a founder of Canada's Catholic New Times and is active in peace and justice work.

Philip McKenna Ph. D. is an Australian, a friend of Gregory Baum's since 1964, and is presently a psychotherapist practicing in Toronto.

Dow Marmur is Rabbi at Holy Blossom Temple in Toronto, Ontario. He is also the author of *Beyond Survival.*

Rosemary Radford Ruether is Georgia Harkness Professor of Theology at Garrett Evangelical Theological Seminary in Evanston, IL. She has written and edited many books in feminist and liberation theology, among them *Sexism and God-Talk* and *Women-Church: Theology and Practice.*

Stephen J. Schäfer is Professor of Social Ethics at Notre Dame Seminary, New Orleans, LA.

Dorothee Sölle is Harry Emerson Fosdick Visiting Professor at Union Theological Seminary in New York. Her most recent book is *To Work and To Love: A theology of creation.*

William M. Thompson is Associate Professor of Theology at Duquesne University in Pittsburgh, PA. His latest work is *Fire and Light: The Saints and Theology.*